VOTING
FOR PRESIDENT

☆
Wallace S. Sayre and Judith H. Parris
☆

VOTING FOR PRESIDENT

The Electoral College and the American Political System

Studies in Presidential Selection
THE BROOKINGS INSTITUTION
Washington, D.C.

Copyright © *1970 by*
THE BROOKINGS INSTITUTION
1775 Massachusetts Avenue, N.W., Washington, D.C. 20036

ISBN 0–8157–7719–1 (paper)
ISBN 0–8157–7720–5 (cloth)

Library of Congress Catalog Card Number 78–139815

THE BROOKINGS INSTITUTION is an independent organization devoted to nonpartisan research, education, and publication in economics, government, foreign policy, and the social sciences generally. Its principal purposes are to aid in the development of sound public policies and to promote public understanding of issues of national importance.

The Institution was founded on December 8, 1927, to merge the activities of the Institute for Government Research, founded in 1916, the Institute of Economics, founded in 1922, and the Robert Brookings Graduate School of Economics and Government, founded in 1924.

The general administration of the Institution is the responsibility of a Board of Trustees charged with maintaining the independence of the staff and fostering the most favorable conditions for creative research and education. The immediate direction of the policies, program, and staff of the Institution is vested in the President, assisted by an advisory committee of the officers and staff.

In publishing a study, the Institution presents it as a competent treatment of a subject worthy of public consideration. The interpretations and conclusions in such publications are those of the author or authors and do not necessarily reflect the views of the other staff members, officers, or trustees of the Brookings Institution.

FOREWORD

THE THREE-WAY presidential contest of 1968 regenerated public interest in a subject that has been of continuing controversy throughout American history—the method of electing the President. This book, the product of a search for expert analysis on the question of how to aggregate the votes in presidential elections, assesses the impact on the American political system of the existing electoral college procedure and hypothesizes about the impact of the several alternative systems that have been proposed.

No justification for such an undertaking is really necessary because it is always in order to reconsider the way the institutions of democratic government function. While Americans take pride in the stability of their institutions and tend to follow a go-slow policy, especially in the matter of formal constitutional amendment, reconsideration does go on, and change does occur. Twentieth century constitutional changes that came from reconsideration include direct election of senators, woman suffrage, and limited presidential tenure. On the other hand, reconsideration of the two-year term of office provided for members of the House of Representatives resulted in retention of the status quo. Clearly enough, the next great constitutional decision will have to do with the future of the electoral college system.

The problem of electoral college reform is not simply of a technical nature. Value judgments are inescapably involved, and reasonable men differ about priorities. The authors offer analysis, but do not hide their judgments or their priorities. To subject analysis and judgments to critical review, a group of leading scholars on political parties and elections was invited to meet at the Brookings Institution, in February 1969, to discuss an earlier version of this manuscript in light of the experience of the 1968 national election. Their comments, which are summarized in an appendix to this volume, are gratefully acknowledged and have been considered in the authors' revisions.

Since the completion of the manuscript of this volume on the electoral college, the Institution has initiated an extended program of studies in presidential selection. These studies will deal with such aspects of the presidential selection system as presidential primaries, national convention management, and the impact of minor parties. A bipartisan national advisory panel of political activists and political journalists provides practical comment and other assistance in the development of the work. While timing precluded involvement of the advisory panel in this study undertaken by Professor Sayre and Mrs. Parris, we have included this book in our series dealing with the problems of presidential selection, where it naturally belongs.

This book continues a Brookings tradition of research on presidential selection. Earlier volumes include *The Politics of National Party Conventions*, by Paul T. David, Ralph M. Goldman, and Richard C. Bain; *The 1956 Presidential Campaign*, by Charles A. H. Thomson and Frances M. Shattuck; *Convention Decisions and Voting Records*, by Richard C. Bain; *Presidential Transitions*, by Laurin L. Henry; *The Presidential Election and Transition, 1960–1961*, edited by Paul T. David; and *The National Election of 1964*, edited by Milton C. Cummings, Jr.

The project was conceived under the general direction of George A. Graham, then director of the Brookings governmental studies program. It was carried out under his successor, Gilbert Y. Steiner. Wallace S. Sayre of Columbia University and Judith H. Parris of Brookings collaborated at long distance—between Washington and the University of London during the senior author's sabbatical year in England. In addition to participants at the Brookings conference of experts, Marjorie Girth of Brookings also read and provided useful comments on the manuscript. Virginia C. Haaga edited the book, and Margaret Stanley prepared the index. Imogene R. Anderson and Caroline Keedy served as secretaries for the project.

As always, the views expressed in this book are the authors', and do not necessarily reflect the views of the trustees, the officers, or other staff members of the Brookings Institution.

KERMIT GORDON
President

July 1970
Washington, D.C.

CONTENTS

VOTING
FOR PRESIDENT

☆

Chapter One

☆

THE ELECTORAL COLLEGE DEBATE

ALEXANDER HAMILTON WROTE IN *The Federalist* of the electoral college system, "I . . . hesitate not to affirm, that if the manner of it be not perfect, it is at least excellent. It unites in an eminent degree all the advantages; the union of which was to be desired." In over 180 years since Hamilton thus endorsed the plan, the electoral college system has invariably produced in forty-six elections a President accepted by the American people and by the political leaders with whom a President must work. In the 145 years since 1825, a President has been chosen without resort to the contingency procedure—election by the House of Representatives. Since 1876 (almost a century) there has been no serious controversy concerning the composition of the electoral college. Since 1888 (over 80 years) the system has always placed in the presidency the candidate with the highest popular vote. By all the ordinary standards of measuring the success of political institutions, then, the electoral college system has an exceptionally good record.

Yet the system has been a quadrennial if not quite a perennial subject of public debate. In large part this is because the election of a President is seen as the most crucial single act in the American political process, overshadowing all other political events; there is understandably a strong urge toward perfection, not just the "excellence" Hamilton called for, in the system in which the act is performed. Accordingly, alternative methods have long had determined advocates. The Constitution-makers in 1787, for example, gave serious consideration to the selection of the President by Congress, but they so convincingly rejected this model of parliamentary government that the idea has not subsequently had much support in the United States. But alternative methods have been proposed. In essence, the debate has turned on different ways of aggregating the votes of the American people for President and Vice President:

—by local districts within each state (the district plan)

—by states (the existing electoral college plan, and the closely related automatic plan)

—by party and by states (the proportional plan)

—by the nation as a whole (the direct-vote plan).

Each of these plans is accompanied by various proposals for changing the contingency election procedure to be used if the first-stage process fails to elect a President. The present system provides that, in these circumstances, the President is to be chosen by the House of Representatives, voting by states. Under other plans that have been proposed, he would be chosen by the House, voting as individual members; or by the House and Senate, voting as individual members in joint session; or by declaring elected the candidate with the most popular or electoral votes; or by popular vote in a national runoff election.

In terms of political impact, only the existing electoral college system is a known quantity. For all the alternatives, we can only speculate about probable and possible consequences. This is an inescapable disability that should concern all who propose to change radically the present system. In so grave a matter the burden of proof lies heavily upon those who would eliminate known defects of the electoral college system but risk the hazards of untested alternatives.

The questions most central to an examination of the leading proposals for changing the method of choosing the President include the following:

Will the method elect the President and Vice President promptly, with infrequent resort to the contingency election procedures?

Will it produce Presidents with an adequate mandate to govern; that is, capable of remaining, as the President has come to be, the mainspring of the American political system?

Will it confer sufficient legitimacy upon the President and the presidency; that is, will it maximize acceptance by citizens and political leaders of the presidential choice?

Will it maintain other established patterns of the American political system:

—The balanced system of separated institutions—President, Congress, Supreme Court—sharing powers?

—The federal system, with the national government, the states, and the localities in a balanced, evolving relationship?

—The national two-party system?

—Political stability during transitions of power, policies, and programs?

John F. Kennedy, then a senator from Massachusetts and a leader in the 1956 debate on the electoral college, put it this way:

> . . . it is not only the unit vote for the Presidency we are talking about, but a whole solar system of governmental power. If it is proposed to change the balance of power of one of the elements of the solar system, it is necessary to consider all the others. . . .
>
> What the effects of these various changes will be on the Federal system, the two-party system, the popular plurality system, and the large-State–small-State checks and balances system, no one knows....
>
> We have no knowledge as to whether these proposed revisions would provide adequate machinery to serve a country in the midst of recurring foreign policy crises—or whether they would lead to a breakdown in this machinery. . . . The world situation does not permit us to take the risk of experimenting with the constitutional system that is fundamental to our strength and leadership . . . without full knowledge of the effects of such changes.[1]

The Authors' Values

Having stated the major considerations that should be weighed, we wish to make clear the values we shall use in weighing them.

1. *Congressional Record*, Vol. 102, Pt. 4, 84 Cong. 2 sess. (1956), pp. 5150, 5156.

As political scientists, we realize that democracy may take many forms, not all of them identical with the contemporary American political system. Great Britain, the "mother of parliaments," has a unitary system rather than the federalism found in the United States. France, Italy, the Scandinavian countries, and many other democracies have multiparty systems. Conceptions of a legitimate popular victory also differ; for example, it was possible in West Germany for Willy Brandt to be chosen chancellor and to rule with a coalition government, even though his party had finished second in the 1969 national election. Many other cases could be cited of deviations from the American norm that are quite compatible with popular control of the government.

However, in evaluating the effects of alternative presidential election arrangements on American politics, we must necessarily choose among the various acceptable patterns that the electoral system may affect. Thus, for the United States we prefer a two-party system to a multiparty system. Aware of the case for the multiparty system—its fuller range of voter choice, its orientation toward issues rather than toward personalities, its satisfactory operation in many nations—we would still oppose its introduction into the United States. We believe that in this vast, diverse nation it is wiser for most of the innumerable interests to group themselves into two great parties and present the electorate finally with a single choice between two national party tickets. We think that this pattern provides not only a moderating atmosphere for the resolution of disputes, many of them at least potentially explosive, but also an efficient basis for administering the government.

We are also believers in a strong presidency. While we do not argue that the government should rule every aspect of American life, or that state and local governments have no important role, or that Congress and the Supreme Court are in the least insignificant, we accept the presidency as the central focus of contemporary American government. We think that the extent of U.S. national commitments and the size of the federal government require a President who can act decisively. We are therefore concerned that the method by which the President is elected should provide him with a strong popular mandate to govern for four years—not as a dictator, not as the weathervane of national opinion, but as an effective executive and national leader, the keystone of the American political system.

We also favor maintaining the federal-state sharing of powers approximately as it now operates and is evolving. Federalism has always been a subject of controversy in American history; the Civil War was fought over the issue. There are some in the United States today who support more state and local autonomy and responsibility; others believe the role of the federal government should be expanded in some areas, including election administration. We think that a strong national government is necessary, just as a strong President is necessary, because of the extent of American national interests and responsibilities. We believe, however, that in a nation of continental size the states have distinct historical and other interests of their own that should be accommodated, within reason, in governing them. We are therefore disposed toward measures that would not seriously disturb the existing balance within the federal system.

Finally, we are concerned about the interests of metropolitan areas and their residents. (By metropolitan areas, we mean both inner cities and suburbs. When we speak subsequently of "cities," and "urban affairs," we shall refer, unless an explicit exception is made, to the inner core areas.) The presidency is the place in the American political system to which residents of the metropolis— and especially the newly emerging minority groups—have the greatest access, except—sometimes—for their own local governments. Whereas state governments, Congress, and the Supreme Court have not been particularly oriented towards metropolitan areas—and have frequently been oriented away from them—the presidency since the New Deal era has been increasingly concerned with the metropolis, in considerable part because of presidential electoral arrangements. We favor this concern, for we believe that the areas where an increasingly predominant percentage of the people live should have effective access to the government.

These, then, are our values, which are intended to conserve the broad pattern of the American political system. There are those who argue that in a time of great social unrest and ferment, such as the time in which we write this book, anyone discussing public policy must be amenable to the reformist urge abroad in the land. According to this school of thought, reluctance to change is mere recalcitrance, unresponsive to the new climate of popular activism summarized in the slogan, "all power to the people." In contrast, we think that one of the unique and perhaps most fortunate attributes of the contemporary electoral reform debate has been its character of moderation. It is not an issue that anyone has been interested in taking to the streets. Instead it has been conducted as the sort of controversy that outside ivy-covered walls is called "academic," despite its political implications—as a matter for reasoned discourse and reflection about the actual effects of alternative methods of electing the President upon American politics. In keeping with that mood, we begin by considering the operation of the presidential election system in the most recent contest, that of 1968.

The Electoral College System

In 1968, a notably bad year for political prophets, it was widely predicted that no one would win the presidency on November 5. This would have occurred had no candidate amassed enough electoral votes to be virtually certain of a majority when the electoral college cast its votes. What actually did occur, of course, was that Richard M. Nixon won a victory in both popular and electoral votes and acceded to the presidency in the usual constitutional way. Why, then, the intense anxiety among some of the nation's most astute political observers?

It is well to begin with the electoral college system itself. Under existing rules, in November of every fourth year, registered voters cast their ballots for slates of electors drawn up by the political parties in each state. When state election officials have tallied the popular vote, all the electors of the slate that has received the most votes are certified as duly elected.[2] In December, the official electors meet in each state and cast separate ballots for President and Vice President. Although they are usually technically free to vote for whomever they please, electors, who are at least quasi-political officers, almost invariably vote for the candidates favored by the voters who elected them as electors; and almost invariably those candidates are the men nominated at their party's national convention. The votes of the state electoral colleges are forwarded to Washington, where they are officially counted by tellers appointed by the House and the Senate; the results are announced by the president of the Senate in a joint session of the new Congress on January 6. If a presidential and a vice presidential candidate have received majorities of the electoral vote, they are declared elected. If not, the President is then chosen by the House of Representatives, voting by states, and the Vice President is chosen by the Senate. Historically, the Senate has performed this duty only once, in 1837; the last time the House chose a President was in 1825. The only deviation from the regular procedure since 1837 came in the disputed election of 1876, when a special commission was appointed by Congress to resolve a controversy over several electors (see Chapter 2).

In 1968 many feared that the House might have to elect a President again—with what they thought might be disastrous results. The principal reason for this concern was the presidential candidacy of former Alabama Governor George C. Wallace on the American Independent party ticket. So long as there are only two

2. Through a law passed in early 1969, Maine is now an exception. Two of the state's four electoral votes go to the ticket carrying the state as a whole; the remaining electoral votes go to the ticket carrying each of its two congressional districts. So long as Maine has four electors, the new system will mean that one vote, at most, could be different from the others.

candidates who have a chance of winning electoral votes, one or the other will almost certainly obtain an electoral majority[3] and thus promptly succeed to the presidency. When a third force enters the picture, however, the arithmetic becomes more complicated. The third force may take any of several forms. Individual electors may bolt and in a close race deny anyone a majority, but historically such dissidents have been extremely few and have never changed the outcome in past elections. Entire slates of major-party electors who vote in the electoral college against both major tickets, as the Mississippi electors did in 1960, have potentially more leverage; but in that year there were not enough to make any difference. A more serious threat might come from a well organized third-party movement with sufficiently concentrated strength to carry several states. That was precisely the George Wallace threat in 1968. Would the Wallace vote be strong enough to preclude an electoral vote majority for anyone else? If so, what then? Would the House be able to choose a President without prolonged conflict that would gravely disrupt the nation's government? Or would Wallace try to keep the choice out of the House, offering to trade his electors for promised concessions on racial matters? Again, would one candidate receive an electoral vote majority but, largely because of the Wallace votes, trail his principal opponent in popular votes? These were the major questions raised by opinion leaders. It seemed to some that the very legitimacy of the American presidency was at stake.

Criticism of the System

The Wallace scare came at a time of increasing criticism of the electoral college system. In late summer, hearings on that topic were published by the Senate subcommittee on constitutional

---

3. Unless there is a tie in electoral votes. There has never been a tie since the Twelfth Amendment, requiring that the electoral college vote for President and Vice President separately, was ratified in 1804. Today, a tie is possible but extremely unlikely.

amendments. The panel had heard testimony in 1966 and 1967 on various proposals to reform the procedure by which the President is elected. Many witnesses had endorsed changes in the system. The American Bar Association (ABA) had restated the conclusions of its Commission on Electoral College Reform, which in January 1967 had produced a report calling the direct-vote plan "the most direct and democratic way of electing a President."[4] The commission added: "The electoral college method of electing a President of the United States is archaic, undemocratic, complex, ambiguous, indirect, and dangerous."[5] Democratic Senator Birch Bayh of Indiana, chairman of the subcommittee, had been converted to a similar view and had introduced an appropriate constitutional amendment. Senator Everett McKinley Dirksen of Illinois, then ranking Republican member of the subcommittee, as well as minority leader of the Senate, announced his support for a similar resolution suggested by the ABA. Most of the scores of resolutions calling for electoral reform introduced during the Ninetieth Congress would have established the direct vote. Press comment took the same line. Polls indicated increasing public support. It appeared that a consensus might be emerging.

Yet there was not complete agreement about the most desirable replacement for the widely criticized existing system. In addition to the direct-vote plan, there were three other leading proposals: the automatic plan, the district plan, and the proportional plan. The automatic plan, which had been sponsored by the Kennedy and Johnson administrations, would have abolished the electoral college and required that a state's total electoral votes be counted for the ticket that carried the state. Reformers had little enthusiasm for that plan, which was essentially a modification of the existing arrangement. Under another plan, the electors' votes would have been counted by specific electoral districts within each state. The district plan was supported mainly by conservative and

4. *Electing the President: A Report of the Commission on Electoral College Reform* (American Bar Association, 1967), p. 4.
5. *Ibid.*, pp. 3–4.

rural forces. Still another plan, then known as the Lodge-Gossett plan, was narrowly defeated in Congress in the 1950s; it called for the abolition of the electoral college and the division of each state's electoral votes among the parties in proportion to the state's popular vote tally. Some Republicans and southern Democrats in 1968 favored the proportional plan; Democratic Senator Sam J. Ervin, Jr., of North Carolina, a key member of the constitutional amendments subcommittee, was one of its principal proponents.

The attentive public was also divided. While the support given by the American Bar Association to the direct-vote plan created the strongest impression about the views of the legal profession, individual leading attorneys testified in favor of alternative plans. Most political scientists who had supported or opposed various reforms in previous years did not take part in the new debate. The AFL-CIO supported the direct vote. The organized business community, notably the United States Chamber of Commerce and the National Association of Manufacturers (NAM), was split between the direct-vote plan and the district plan. The former organization was willing to accept either plan; the NAM supported the district plan.

None of the plans discussed came to a vote. Indeed, the Ninetieth Congress could not change the rules of the 1968 contest. Any solution to problems had to be worked out within the existing system.

The Orfield Plan

One such solution was devised by Gary Orfield, a political scientist at the University of Virginia. He suggested an agreement from both parties—by their candidates, in their platforms, and by their congressional leaders—pledging that they would not in any circumstances bargain with George Wallace.[6]

To this end, Representatives Charles E. Goodell, Republican of

6. Gary Orfield, "A Proposal for Outfoxing Wallace," *Washington Post*, July 7, 1968, p. B-2.

New York, and Morris K. Udall, Democrat of Arizona, began circulating a petition among House members committing their votes to the winner of the popular vote plurality if election of the President should devolve upon the House. A counterpart group was established in the Senate, pledging votes for the popular winner for Vice President if the contest went to their chamber. The presidential nominees, Richard Nixon and Hubert Humphrey, publicly declared that they would not bargain with Wallace. However, the Republican and Democratic conventions failed to incorporate any specific commitment in their platforms, calling instead for some sort of electoral college reform. And as election time drew near, many congressmen, particularly southerners who anticipated a strong Wallace vote at home, began to express their desire to vote, if the election went to the House, for the candidate who had carried their local districts. The House leaders did not endorse the Orfield plan; the press quoted Republican leaders as encouraging their doubtful partisans to vote their districts rather than their national party if the occasion arose.[7]

The 1968 Contest Gets Close

As November approached, the tide of the campaign began to turn. Wallace began to lose ground, Humphrey began to gain, and Nixon stayed about the same. By election day, both the outcome of the popular vote and the likelihood of an electoral vote majority were definitely in doubt. Polls taken the weekend before the election by both Harris and Gallup had given Nixon 42 percent of the popular vote, Humphrey 40 percent, and Wallace less than 15 percent.[8] On election eve a last-minute Harris poll was published showing Humphrey with a popular lead of 43 percent to Nixon's 40 percent. None of the national polls, however, was taken in such

7. "GOP Congressmen Freed to Vote for Wallace in House Showdown," *Washington Post*, Sept. 26, 1968, p. A-10.
8. *Washington Post*, Nov. 4, 1968, p. A-1.

a way as to shed light on the probable outcome of the electoral vote. Nixon, who was generally expected to win more popular votes, urged that the House choose the popular-vote winner, if it were called upon to decide. At the same time he said that the entire electoral system should be overhauled and reiterated his support for the proportional plan. Humphrey, anticipating that the House would be Democratically controlled, supported the existing constitutional procedures.

Network television and radio coverage of the 1968 election returns probably made ordinary American citizens more aware of the electoral college than they had ever been before. Traditionally, the networks had kept counts of the electoral vote as well as the popular vote as returns were available. In recent elections, computers have been fed increasingly sophisticated sets of data in order to arrive at increasingly reliable projections of outcomes. This coverage was expanded in 1968; because of the closeness of the race, the electoral college system was explained repeatedly. Virtually every conceivable way that the candidate with the most popular votes might lose the election was noted and discussed at length.

As their colleagues on newspapers and magazines had been doing for many weeks, newsmen on the various networks offered assessments of the electoral college system; most emphasized what they considered to be its faults, particularly the potential leverage it had given to the George Wallace candidacy. Several leading commentators expressed their support for direct election. Theodore White was a dissenter. He noted the failure of several hundred precincts in Illinois and Texas to post returns as quickly as the rest of their states, and he argued that the direct-vote plan would mean turning the election over to what he called the crooks who administer elections in many localities. In a close election, he contended, they would create a profound problem of uncertainty— not only in the United States, but throughout the world—about the outcome of the election. However, this was a minority view. Most comment was critical of the opportunity for political maneuvering that Wallace appeared to have.

The Election Outcome

These fears were not realized. By mid-morning on November 6, it was clear that Richard Nixon had carried some thirty-two states with 302 electoral votes and achieved a popular margin over Hubert Humphrey of nearly 500,000 votes. The GOP ticket received 43.4 percent of the popular vote, the Democrats 42.7 percent, and George Wallace 13.5 percent. Wallace's popular percentage was less than both Theodore Roosevelt's 27.4 percent as a Bull Moose candidate in 1912 and Robert LaFollette's 16.6 percent as a Progressive in 1924. For all the furor, Wallace ultimately did only slightly better under the electoral college system than Senator J. Strom Thurmond had done in 1948. Wallace's 13.5 percent of the popular total was far better than the 2.4 percent won by Thurmond, who unlike Wallace was on the ballot in only a handful of states. Of the electoral votes, however, Wallace won 46 (some 8.6 percent of the total), and Thurmond won 39 (7.3 percent). One electoral college vote for Wallace came from a defecting North Carolina Republican; one for Thurmond had come from a defecting Tennessean.

Richard Nixon amassed a larger popular vote plurality than had John F. Kennedy when he won the 1960 presidential race. Because of the Wallace vote, Nixon's popular percentage, 43.5, was not as good as Kennedy's 49.5; but his plurality of 500,000 was well above Kennedy's 112,000. In addition, Nixon carried more states —thirty-two to Kennedy's twenty-four. (The latter figure includes Alabama, although some of the Democratic electors of that state did not vote for Kennedy in the electoral college.)

The Nixon electoral vote majority, which was predictable from the popular returns available on November 6, was sufficiently strong that any maneuvering in the electoral college appeared futile and hence unlikely. The identity of the President-elect was clear.

The outcome would probably have been far less certain under most proposed substitutes for the electoral college system. With the *direct-vote* plan in effect, the President- and Vice President-elect would have been the men with the highest popular total, provided they had received at least 40 percent of the ballots cast. Because of the narrow popular margin and the delay in tallying absentee ballots, a national recount might have been necessary. Indecision, considerable confusion, and an even longer time for counting the returns would have resulted under the *district* or *proportional* plans. The former plan would have required that returns be tallied within each electoral district and that a nationwide total then be made. Under the proportional plan, calculations (to three decimal places) of each party's share of each state's electoral votes would have been required; no count would be reliable until the last absentee ballot was in and the last recount had been made. In either case the outcome would have been in doubt for quite some time. Only under the *automatic* plan, which provides for aggregating the votes as at present, would the decision have been as clear as quickly as it in fact was.

The Congressional Response

Concern about the Wallace candidacy overshadowed the functional effectiveness of the electoral system in producing a President and Vice President in 1968. Senator Bayh held a news conference on November 8 at which he announced his intention to continue to fight for the direct-vote plan. This plan, Bayh said, would "give [the people] a voice; now they don't have a voice." Democratic Congressman Hale Boggs of Louisiana, House majority whip, said he would introduce an automatic plan. Democratic Congressman Emanuel Celler of New York, chairman of the House Judiciary Committee, said his panel would also hold early hearings on electoral reform.

The public seemed ready for reform. In a Harris poll taken the week before the election and published November 11, respondents were asked how they viewed election by the House "if the electoral college can't elect a President." Some 24 percent favored the procedure, 60 percent opposed it, and 16 percent were undecided.

When asked whether they would prefer that the candidate with a popular plurality be named President if there were no electoral college majority, or whether they favored negotiations among the candidates in the electoral college, some 72 percent said the former, 14 percent the latter, and 14 percent were undecided.[9] The American Institute of Public Opinion asked voters before and after the election: "Would you approve or disapprove of an amendment to the Constitution which would do away with the Electoral College and base the election of a President on the total vote cast throughout the Nation?" Before the election, 66 percent approved; after the election, 81 percent approved. Opposition dropped from 19 percent to 12 percent and the undecided vote from 15 percent to 7 percent.[10] The question, of course, incorrectly implied that the verdict of the electoral college is not based on the popular vote.

Much of the press, which had helped form the public view of the electoral college, was also reform-minded. The *New York Times*, the *Washington Post*, and other leading publications endorsed the direct-vote plan.

Congress moved expeditiously in response to such sentiment. Democratic Senator and 1968 vice presidential candidate Edmund S. Muskie of Maine and Democratic Representative James G. O'Hara of Michigan led a movement to challenge the electoral college vote cast for George Wallace by a Republican elector from North Carolina, Dr. Lloyd W. Bailey. On January 6, 1969, the resolution to set aside the Bailey vote was rejected by the Senate, 58–33, and by the House, 229–169. The day-long debate, however, dramatized the cause of electoral reform.

The cause was also discussed in a more conventional fashion. The House Judiciary Committee heard testimony on the issue in February and March. The Senate subcommittee on constitutional amendments held similar hearings during January, March, April, and May. Before both panels, most witnesses—the American Bar Association, the AFL-CIO, the American Civil Liberties Union,

9. *Ibid.*, Nov. 11, 1968, p. A-25.
10. *Ibid.*, Nov. 24, 1968, p. A-2.

and others from the liberal-labor bloc—urged passage of a direct-vote amendment. The principal reasons given were that the direct-vote plan would ensure the election of the popular plurality winner and would obviate political wheeling and dealing by a minor party candidate like George Wallace or a "faithless" elector like Dr. Bailey. The existing electoral college system was also criticized as unduly complicated, difficult for citizens to understand, and biased in favor of urban areas and populous states.

There was some dissent from the direct-vote sentiment. Attorney General John N. Mitchell told the House committee that while President Nixon favored the direct-vote principle, the administration had informally polled state legislators and concluded that such an amendment would never be accepted by the requisite three-fourths of the states. Accordingly, Mitchell explained, the administration would not actively support a specific plan but would back any reform measure passed by Congress. In addition, some conservative and right-wing witnesses at the hearings—ranging from the American Farm Bureau Federation to elector Lloyd Bailey and the Liberty Lobby—supported the district plan. The proportional plan, which was nearly approved by Congress in the 1950s, aroused little interest. And few of those who testified defended the existing electoral vote system; those who did, endorsed the automatic plan. This last group included the National Association for the Advancement of Colored People, which refused to support the direct-vote plan until the right of all citizens to vote was, in its view, adequately guaranteed; the American Jewish Congress, which was concerned about possible adverse effects of the direct vote on the two-party system and on other factors; and men like Congressman Hale Boggs, who leaned toward the direct-vote plan but did not think it could be adopted.

The House Judiciary Committee approved a direct-vote amendment by a 29–6 margin on April 29. The committee report said that abolition of the electoral college would "remove an artificial, intermediate step in determining the people's choice of a popular leader." The going was more difficult in the Senate Judiciary Committee. In May the divided Bayh subcommittee agreed to recommend a district plan as a means of getting the issue into the full committee. But the parent group became enmeshed in the nomination of Judge Clement F. Haynsworth to the Supreme Court, and the question of electoral reform was postponed until the session of Congress opening in January 1970.

Meanwhile, the House Rules Committee held hearings on the amendment[11] approved by the House Judiciary Committee. On July 24, 1969, the panel granted the measure an open rule with six hours of floor debate, which began on September 9. Judiciary Chairman Emanuel Celler served as manager for the measure, which provided in essence for a direct-vote plan that required the winning presidential ticket to carry at least 40 percent of the popular vote; if none did, there would be a runoff popular election between the top two.

Throughout the House debate, proponents of the direct-vote plan stressed the measure's democratic thrust and the possible dangers inherent in the electoral college system. Some fifteen amendments were considered during the six days of debate. Notable among them were amendments providing for substitution of the district, proportional, and automatic plans for the direct-vote plan; a measure increasing, and a measure decreasing, the plurality required for a candidate to win; an amendment providing for ratification by special state conventions instead of by the state legislatures; one providing for congressional standards for voter qualifications and access of candidates to the ballot; and an amendment substituting a joint session of Congress for the runoff procedure to choose the President if no ticket received 40 percent of the popular vote. All the amendments were defeated except one, proposed by Republican Representative Richard H. Poff of Virginia and accepted by Representative Celler, that added "inability" to a clause covering the death or withdrawal of candidates.

The House passed the direct-vote amendment on September 18, 1969, by a 339–70 margin, considerably more than the two-thirds vote required. On September 30, President Nixon endorsed the

11. H.J. Res. 681, *Congressional Record*, daily ed., Sept. 11, 1969, p. H7823.

amendment in a formal statement, saying: "Because the ultimate goal of electoral reform must prevail over differences as to how best to achieve that goal, I endorse the direct election approach and urge the Senate also to adopt it."[12]

The Senate moved cautiously. In April 1970 its Judiciary Committee held further electoral reform hearings at which more testimony critical of the direct-vote plan was heard than in the earlier Bayh subcommittee hearings. One witness was freshman Democratic Senator Thomas F. Eagleton of Missouri, who urged adoption of the "federal system plan" that he and freshman Republican Senator Robert Dole of Kansas had introduced on March 5. Their amendment[13] provided for a direct-vote plan with election of the plurality winner if he carried (1) more than half the states, or (2) a plurality in states with over half the voters, or (3) a majority of the electoral votes, awarded on a state general-ticket basis. If there were still no winner, the electoral votes won by minor candidates would be allocated to the top two contestants in proportion to their showing in each state; and the electoral vote majority winner would be declared President.

This compromise, however, was unsuccessful in the committee, which approved the Bayh amendment by an 11–6 vote on April 23. Various other proposals had been offered and voted down, some by narrow margins. An automatic plan lost, 9–7; a proportional plan lost, 9–8. A plan similar to the Eagleton-Dole measure, introduced by Democratic Senator Joseph D. Tydings of Maryland and Republican Senator Robert P. Griffin of Michigan, was defeated, 10–6.

The Electoral College and the American Political System

In spite of all this activity, the debate about electoral reform has been curiously shallow. There has been little systematic examination of the likely effects of proposed reform measures. Nor has the

12. *New York Times*, Oct. 1, 1969, p. 18.
13. S.J. Res. 181, *Congressional Record*, daily ed., March 5, 1970, pp. S3027–28.

current debate provided a balanced appraisal of the existing system. The consensus has developed that the direct vote is progressive and the electoral college archaic—a conclusion that grossly oversimplifies the significance of both for American politics. The way the American President is selected is not a minor question of mechanics.

This book represents an attempt to analyze more fully the changes that have been proposed for the electoral college system. Is the existing procedure the best for electing the President of the United States? Or does the twentieth century require a system different from that devised by the founding fathers in an earlier and quite different age? The approach used here is based on three assumptions. First, it is assumed that in policy making all the conceivable relevant effects of alternative proposals ought to be thoroughly studied. Here the principal evidence will be the existing knowledge about American politics. Second, it is assumed that the machinery of a political system is not neutral; it serves the advantages of some and causes disadvantages to others. Finally, it is assumed that the office of the presidency and its constituency are both so important that the way in which the chief executive is chosen is one of the major underpinnings of the American political system.

To repeat, the debate over the electoral college is not a debate over whether the President should be elected by the popular vote of the American people. The present system and all the seriously considered alternatives have long rested on a popular vote. Rather, the debate is over how the popular vote should be aggregated: whether by state subdivisions (as in the district plan), or by states (as in the existing electoral college system and in the automatic plan), or by party vote by states (as in the proportional plan), or by the nation as a whole (as in the direct-vote plan). Each of these choices involves significant consequences for American politics, including particularly the nature of the party system, the office of the presidency, the balance of power between metropolitan and nonmetropolitan areas, and the federal structure.

Accordingly, this book discusses how the presidential electoral system has worked and the probable effects of the various proposed changes. The next chapter describes historical developments related to the electoral college, beginning with the Constitutional Convention of 1787. Subsequent chapters, in turn, deal with the existing system and the four leading alternatives. The final chapter records the authors' conclusions about what method seems best for today and tomorrow.

☆

Chapter Two

☆

THE HISTORICAL SETTING

THE ELECTORAL COLLEGE SYSTEM has a history of nearly two hundred years. Its basic rules were written by the founding fathers of the republic and have been formally amended only once. Yet time has brought great changes in the system and in public attitudes toward it. Outcomes of various elections have affected both the way subsequent Presidents have been chosen and public discussions about the method of choice. Patterns in the selection of electors have shifted through time in accordance with changing political norms. Various reform proposals have been made and studied. The franchise has been greatly extended since 1789. These evolving factors, in combination, are of considerable significance to the current debate.

The Constitutional Convention

The method of electing the President was only one issue facing the men who met in Philadelphia in 1787. They came originally to amend the Articles of Confederation, under whose charter their young nation had operated haltingly since the end of the Revolutionary War. The Articles, allowing wide leeway for individual state autonomy, provided minimal central government. Congress, as Clinton Rossiter has written, "could resolve and recommend but could not command and coerce."[1] Domestic upheavals, like Shays's rebellion in Massachusetts, and fears of foreign interven-

1. Clinton Rossiter, *1787: The Grand Convention* (Macmillan, 1966), p. 52.

tion on the North American continent encouraged moves to strengthen the national regime. Accordingly, representatives of Virginia, Pennsylvania, Delaware, New Jersey, and New York gathered at Annapolis in 1786 and called for a convocation of delegates from all the states to meet in Philadelphia the following May to propose revisions in the Articles. Congress echoed the call, and preparations began.

The central achievement of the convention was to hammer out a compromise which provided as much strengthening of the national government as the states would accept. The thirteen former colonies were quite jealous of their hard-won independence and their virtual autonomy. Even the procedure for forging a new union reflected the power of the individual states. Each delegate was a representative of his state; states voted as units within the convention; and the document produced had to be ratified by at least nine states before it could go into effect. Yet the predominant tone of the convention was, in the context of its time, nationalist. Early in the meeting, on May 30, a resolution was passed by a 6–1 vote calling for the creation of a national government consisting of a supreme legislature, executive, and judiciary. Once this direction had been established, it was never changed.[2] The Great Compromise—equal representation of states in the Senate and representation according to population in the House—symbolized the balancing of new national and old state interests.

Thinking on the presidency was mixed. There was distrust of potential tyranny from power centralized in any single institution. A strong executive was particularly reminiscent of unpopular colonial governors, and even English kings. At the same time, at least equally widespread among delegates was a conviction that the "executive" under the Articles was virtually a cipher and must be strengthened. Many believed that running the affairs of the United States almost entirely by a collegial body—the Congress— was inefficient and unwise. Hence the convention declared that

2. *Ibid.*, p. 172.

"the Executive Power shall be vested in a President of the United States of America. . . ."

The method for electing the President was a vexing issue. As James Wilson, a leading delegate from Pennsylvania, put it: "This subject has greatly divided the house, and will also divide people out of doors. It is in truth the most difficult of all on which we have had to decide."[3] Although various schemes were proposed, in essence three were considered in various combinations: election by Congress, election by the people, and election by the state governments. The convention formally considered several plans and rejected them all. The whole question of the presidency was then referred to a committee on postponed matters. This committee decided that the President should be elected by a group of electors chosen in each state as its legislature should direct. The number of each state's electors would be the same as its representation in Congress; they would meet in their states and cast ballots for two persons each for President, at least one of whom is not a resident of their state. The votes would then be sent to the Senate to be counted; the candidate with a majority of the votes would become President, and the runner-up would become Vice President. If no one had a majority, the Senate would choose the President from among the five with the most votes; the man with the second most votes would be Vice President. But many delegates believed that once George Washington, the obvious choice for first President, had passed from the scene, few candidates would obtain electoral vote majorities. Thus, they feared that the Senate would frequently elect the President and perhaps even control him. Therefore, the convention accepted an amendment substituting the House—generally believed to be the weaker chamber and also the one closer to the people—as the body to choose the President if no candidate received an electoral majority. The House was to vote by states, as the delegates to the Philadelphia convention themselves did.

3. Max Farrand, *Records of the Federal Convention of 1787* (Yale University Press, 1937), Vol. 2, p. 501.

The system that was finally devised, like the total product of the convention, was a compromise among various forces and suggestions. "Everybody got a piece of the cake," one historian has noted.[4] Congress was expected to have a hand in the electoral procedure frequently. The method of choosing electors was left up to the states; often they were appointed by the state legislature. The people might choose their state electors if their legislatures so decided. The executive would be far stronger than under the Articles, but it would not be completely independent of Congress. Small and large states would retain in the electoral college the same relative benefits they had under the congressional representation arrangement: a minimum of three votes for each state, even the smallest, with additional votes based on population.

Ratification

Once the draft Constitution had been approved by the convention, it was referred to the states. Months of struggle ensued within the thirteen state legislatures. At length, on June 21, 1788, the ninth state, New Hampshire, ratified the Constitution, thus achieving the necessary majority of states to bring about union. The last state, Rhode Island, ratified in 1790. George Washington had been duly elected and sworn in as President the year before.

The electoral college was apparently not discussed very much during the debates over ratification. Emphasis was placed on larger issues, principally the comparative merits of the planned union and the existing confederation. Everyone expected Washington to be the first President in any case.

The fullest major contemporary discussion of the electoral college now extant is found in *The Federalist*, No. 68, generally attributed to Alexander Hamilton.[5] "The mode of appointment of

---

4. John P. Roche, "The Electoral College: A Note on American Political Mythology," *Dissent* (Spring 1961), p. 198.

5. Jacob E. Cooke, ed., *The Federalist* (World Publishing Co., 1961), pp. 437–62. All quotations are from No. 68.

the chief magistrate of the United States," he begins, "is almost the only part of the system, of any consequence, which has escaped without severe censure." This fact, Hamilton continues, demonstrates the viability of the system. He documents his case for the electoral college system point by point. Since "the sense of the people should operate," they choose the electors, at least indirectly. Electors make the actual choice because they "will be most likely to possess the information and discernment requisite" to pick a good President. Having a body of electors, rather than a single man, and voting by electors in geographically isolated state groups rather than as an assembled body, Hamilton adds, affords "as little opportunity as possible to tumult and disorder." Corruption, and especially foreign intrigue, he continues, are discouraged by a specifically designated electoral college, from which public officeholders are expressly excluded. In addition, the President is kept "independent for his continuance in office on all, but the people themselves." Hence, he will be mindful of his duty, rather than the pressure of others. Such a system, Hamilton contends, will assure that statesmen, and not demagogues, are elected President: "Talents for low intrigue, and the little arts of popularity, may alone suffice to elevate a man to the first honours of a single state; but it will require other talents, and a different kind of merit, to establish him in the esteem and confidence of the whole union. . . ."

Evolution of the Electoral College System

Once established, the electoral college system adapted itself to the emergent political party system and the rising ideal of electoral democracy. Other practical adaptations were also made. By the end of the nineteenth century, the structure devised in 1789 had been formally amended only once; but the working system was far different from that originally envisioned. A review of the period shows the dimensions of the change.

At first the electoral college appeared to work well. In 1789 and 1792, as expected, George Washington was elected President by the unanimous vote of the electors. Trouble began with the emergence, somewhat unexpectedly, of nascent national political parties in the election of 1796. That year, a Federalist—John Adams—had a majority in the electoral college, and a Republican—Thomas Jefferson—had the second most votes. Accordingly, under existing constitutional rules, they were elected President and Vice President, respectively. The undesirability of a President of one persuasion and a Vice President of another soon became obvious.

The 1796 election also marked the beginning of a recurrent, but minor, partisan problem in the electoral college system. For the first time, an elector bolted the ticket to which he was pledged; one of the two Federalist electors from Pennsylvania cast his vote for Thomas Jefferson. An angry Federalist voiced the irritation of his fellow partisans: "What, do I chuse Samuel Miles to determine for me whether John Adams or Thomas Jefferson shall be President? No! I chuse him to *act*, not to *think*."[6] This distinction focused on the core of subsequent debates about the proper role of presidential electors. But Samuel Miles's defection did not cost John Adams the election; he received 71 votes from the 138 electors. Miles set an informal precedent—followed by five subsequent electors through 1968 who bolted the ticket but had no practical effect on the outcome except for the alarm their action created.

Far more serious were the effects of political parties on the operation of the electoral college in 1800. As party loyalty demanded, the Republican electors chosen cast seventy-three votes for Thomas Jefferson, the Republican candidate for President, and for Aaron Burr, the party's vice presidential candidate. This was a majority of the 138 electoral votes; but because there was no formal designation as to whether Jefferson or Burr was to be President, they were in fact tied. The contest was thrown into the House, where some Federalists were willing to support Burr in exchange for promises of later favors. Alexander Hamilton, a

6. Quoted by Neal R. Peirce in *The People's President* (Simon & Schuster, 1968), p. 64.

leading Federalist, urged support for Jefferson—an old antagonist but, in Hamilton's view, a more honorable man than the unreliable Burr. For reasons that are unclear to historians, Burr himself did not take full advantage of his opportunity. There was a Federalist majority in the House; but the outcome there was uncertain because in choosing the President the House was required to cast its votes by state delegations and not as individuals. After six days and thirty-six ballots the House elected Jefferson by a vote of ten states to four.

This direct experience of protracted indecision made reform imperative. Various plans were suggested, some of which had been offered even before the election. In March 1800, for example, Representative John Nicholas of Virginia had introduced a proposal calling for the establishment of electoral districts within each state for choosing presidential electors. Alexander Hamilton on May 7 of the same year had urged Governor John Jay of New York to reconvene a lame-duck Federalist legislature, persuade them to enact a district plan, and hence deprive Jefferson of New York's votes in November; Jay opposed the move as unduly partisan. President Jefferson himself, obviously affected by the threat of faithless electors to his own career, in a letter to Albert Gallatin in 1801 discussed a plan by which "the people vote directly, and the ticket which has a plurality of the votes in any state is considered as receiving the whole vote of the state."[7]

The Twelfth Amendment, which was adopted in 1804, was more modest. It provided simply that electors should vote separately for President and Vice President and that the presidential candidate with a majority was to be President and the vice presidential candidate with a majority was to be Vice President. If no one obtained a majority, the House, voting by state delegations, was to elect the President "from the persons having the highest numbers not exceeding three on the list of those voted for as President"; the Senate was to elect the Vice President from the top two

7. Quoted in Lucius Wilmerding, *The Electoral College* (Rutgers University Press, 1958), p. 170.

candidates for that office. If the House could not agree, the Vice President-elect, whose age, citizenship, and residence requirements were made the same as the President's, was to serve as acting President.

Satisfaction with the essentially technical change involved in the Twelfth Amendment was not universal. Many states, over time, changed their methods of choosing electors. At first, various systems were used: appointment by the state legislature, election from local districts, the winner-take-all state general-ticket system, and mixed patterns. By 1836 South Carolina was the only state that did not use the general-ticket system. Political leaders realized that if one state chose its electors by this system—a state unit vote for a single slate—then other states must also adopt the system in order to prevent diminution of their strength relative to that of other states. South Carolina adopted the general ticket in 1860, and it has since been standard operating procedure throughout the country, with few exceptions.

There were also various attempts at the national level to establish a uniform method of voting for the President, necessarily by means of a constitutional amendment. Proposals ranged from choice by lot through the direct-vote plan. In 1813 the Senate approved a district plan by a 22–9 vote; the House failed to act. In 1816 Senator Abner Lacock of Pennsylvania proposed the first direct-vote plan amendment; it lost by a vote of 12 to 21. In 1818 a majority of senators—but not the requisite two-thirds majority— approved a district plan. In 1819 the Senate passed another such measure by a 28–10 vote; again the House failed to act. The next year the Senate again approved the amendment, and the House mustered a majority of 92 to 54, just short of the two-thirds margin needed. The district plan has never since come so close to passage in Congress.

Meanwhile, a body of customs began to develop around the electoral college as an institution. The early nineteenth century brought the first congressional challenges to the electoral votes cast by the states. In 1809 Massachusetts's votes were challenged;

in 1817, Indiana's; and in 1820, Missouri's. Congress rejected all the challenges. A precedent was thus set that Congress would not "go behind the returns" certified by state officials.

Again, in 1820 former New Hampshire Senator William Plumer, who was an elector pledged to James Monroe, voted in the electoral college for John Quincy Adams, whom he considered a better man. This second "faithless" elector followed the pattern of the first in 1796. His defection made no difference: Monroe, running in the Era of Good Feelings, received 231 electoral votes out of a possible 232.

The year 1824, in contrast, was a watershed in the history of presidential elections. In an intervening period of factionalism—between the Jeffersonian and Jacksonian two-party systems—four candidates received electoral college votes, but none obtained a majority. Andrew Jackson received 99 votes; John Quincy Adams, 84; William Crawford, 41; and Henry Clay, 37. When, as then prescribed by statute, the outgoing House voted for President (it would be the incoming House today), Adams won thirteen states to Jackson's seven. Complete returns are not available, since there was no popular vote in six states where the legislature chose electors; but of the recorded popular votes, Adams got only 31.9 percent to Jackson's 42.2 percent.[8] As a result of the 1824 election, Andrew Jackson became bitterly opposed to the electoral college and called for its abolition in every State of the Union message after his election to the presidency in 1828. More important, there was widespread public criticism, particularly of the possibility of a discrepancy between popular and electoral votes. This was an important issue in an age when frontier democracy was a leading progressive force.

Yet the 1824 election controversy was not enough to generate fundamental electoral reform. In 1826 the district plan was brought to a vote once more in the House, where the vote was 102 to 90—again less than the necessary two-thirds majority. In the same year Representative Charles E. Haynes of Georgia intro-

8. All popular vote figures are taken from Peirce, *op. cit.*, pp. 304–07.

duced the first version of what came to be known as the automatic plan—the automatic casting of all of a state's electoral college votes for the candidates who carried the popular vote in the state. This measure was also unsuccessful.

Again, there was little stir when in 1837 the Senate, for the first and thus far the only time, was called upon to choose the Vice President. Richard M. Johnson, running mate of the Democratic presidential winner, Martin Van Buren, did not receive the vote of the Virginia Democratic electors and hence lacked an electoral vote majority. The Senate chose him by a vote of 33 to 16. Political reaction to the use of the contingency election procedure was negligible.

During the crisis of secession in 1860 the winning presidential candidate received the smallest percentage of the total popular vote ever. Abraham Lincoln, who was not on the ballot in ten states, got only 39.8 percent of the popular total in a four-man race. Except possibly in the South, he was accepted by his countrymen as the legitimate President. Even in the South, his unpopularity was based on the slavery issue rather than on the extent of his electoral support. Others who were elected President during the nineteenth century with majorities of the electoral vote but not of the popular vote were also considered legitimate winners: James K. Polk with 49.6 percent of the popular vote in 1844; Zachary Taylor with 47.3 percent in 1848; James Buchanan with 45.6 percent in 1856; James A. Garfield with 48.3 percent in 1880; and Grover Cleveland with 48.5 percent in 1884 and 48.6 percent in 1892. No substantial objection to their assuming power followed their narrow victories. A President who won with an electoral majority and a popular plurality was apparently acceptable to most Americans.

Nonetheless, there was some discontent with the electoral college system. Various reform proposals were put forward, including the first call for a proportional division of each state's electoral college votes by party. This was sponsored by Representative William T. Lawrence of New York in 1848. None of these measures came to a formal vote. President Andrew Johnson, who had introduced a similar proposal as a congressman in the 1850s, sent Congress a message in 1868 calling for the direct-vote plan. No action was taken on it. However, the popular vote was extended to nonwhite men when the Fifteenth Amendment was ratified in 1870.

In 1872 the problem of a candidate's death became a real one. Horace Greeley, the Democratic nominee for President, died between the November election, when he lost overwhelmingly, both in actual popular votes and in probable electoral votes, and the December electoral college meetings. The Constitution did not cover this possibility. Democratic electors scattered their votes among the various other candidates.

For political drama, the presidential election of 1876 was the equal of those of 1800 and 1824. Democrat Samuel J. Tilden won 50.9 percent of the popular vote, as officially recorded, and Republican Rutherford B. Hayes, 47.9 percent. Yet Hayes was the man who moved into the White House. At the time, federal troops were still occupying three southern states, which were being governed by Republican reconstruction officials. It appeared that Tilden had won the election, but votes were contested in Louisiana, South Carolina, and Florida. The Republican ticket was declared the winner in those states by (Republican) state election officials. In addition, Democrats in Oregon had challenged a Republican elector in that state who was also a deputy postmaster and thus constitutionally ineligible to serve. But he resigned his federal job, the Republicans reappointed him, and Hayes won all of Oregon's votes. This gave Hayes a lead in the electoral college of 185 to 184.

As furious Democrats protested the vote, Congress enacted legislation creating a special electoral commission, appointed by President Ulysses S. Grant, to investigate the dispute. Tilden argued that the commission was illegal because the House had the power to decide in cases of disputed returns. Tilden's case also had partisan overtones, for the Democrats controlled the House. The commission proceeded and, making use of congressional precedent, said it could not go beyond the returns and investigate fraud. At length it voted on straight party lines, 8 to 7, that Hayes had been duly elected by the electoral college. The decision was generally accepted by the public, although many Democrats continued to contend that they had been robbed.

In 1888 the legitimacy of the electoral vote system was directly tested. Benjamin Harrison won an electoral college majority but received fewer popular votes than did his opponent, Grover Cleveland. Harrison got 5,445,269 votes (47.8 percent) and Cleveland 5,540,365 (48.6 percent). Harrison carried more of the large, competitive states with major blocs of electoral votes. There were rumors of voting irregularities, which were certainly credible considering the times. Cleveland, an incumbent President, might have intervened in the regular transition of power. Yet nothing of the kind happened. Cleveland and his fellow countrymen accepted the verdict of the system.

The Twentieth Century

Over the current century, criticism of the electoral college system has increased, particularly when minor parties and dissident southerners have threatened to create a "crisis." The principal concern of reformers has been that the man with the most popular votes win—a natural concern during an era that began with the Progressive movement, brought vastly extended suffrage and concern for voting rights, and included several very close presidential elections. Yet the electoral college system that was developed by the end of the nineteenth century has functioned basically without incident up to the present; and in the twentieth century the candidate with the most votes has always won.

The four-way presidential race in 1912, among Democrat Woodrow Wilson, incumbent Republican William Howard Taft, Progressive Theodore Roosevelt, and Socialist Eugene V. Debs, generated wide discussion of the electoral system. Many believed that no candidate would win a majority in the electoral college and that the contest would thus go to the House. Political leaders devised alternative strategies for various contingencies. For example, the Roosevelt slate in South Dakota declared that if it were elected and Roosevelt could not win in the electoral college, it would vote for Taft in order to defeat Wilson. But Wilson, although he carried only 41.9 percent of the popular vote, won handily with 435 electoral college votes. For this reason, the death of the Republican Vice President, James S. Sherman, who was running for reelection, did not affect the election significantly. The Republican National Committee simply instructed the party's eight electors to cast their votes for Columbia University president Nicholas Murray Butler.

Discussion of the electoral college issue continued only sporadically in the 1920s and 1930s, when none of the presidential elections was close. In 1923 the House held hearings on electoral college reform, but no action was taken. In 1933 a House committee reported a proportional plan, but the measure never reached a floor vote. The Senate Judiciary Committee reported an automatic plan, which was brought to a vote on the floor on May 21, 1934; the vote was 42 to 24 in favor of the plan, but this was less than the necessary two-thirds majority.

In 1941 Republican Senator Henry Cabot Lodge of Massachusetts introduced a proportional plan that was to be the focus of electoral reform debates through the 1950s. The Lodge resolution and a companion House measure were favorably reported out of committee in 1944, but no floor votes were taken. In 1948 the Senate again held hearings on the proportional plan, this time sponsored by Senator Lodge and Democratic Representative Ed Gossett of Texas; the measure was not reported in either chamber that year. In 1949 both houses held hearings, and committees reported the Lodge-Gossett plan. Floor votes came the following year. The Senate in 1950 rejected an automatic plan by a 20–71 vote. It also twice defeated a direct-vote plan, first by a 31–60 vote when it was included in a bill that provided for presidential primaries and then by a vote of 28 to 63 on its own merits. Support for the proportional plan was at its height when the Senate approved the Lodge-Gossett amendment by a 64–27 margin. But on the House side, a coalition of northern Democrats and Republicans kept the measure bottled up in the Rules Committee. At length, Congressman Gossett moved to suspend the rules and pass his measure. His motion lost, 134 to 210. During the next year the Lodge-Gossett amendment was again reported in both houses but never brought to a vote.

Meanwhile, a new and serious problem concerning the electoral college developed during this era as Democrats in certain southern states who opposed the race relations policies of their national party tried to withhold their electoral votes from the national ticket. Thus, in Texas in 1944, forces opposed to President Franklin D. Roosevelt controlled the state convention and urged the state's electors to vote against FDR in December. A group of pro-Roosevelt Texans bolted the convention and established a rump group pledged to the President. Congressman Lyndon B. Johnson tried to mediate between the factions. Democratic leaders in other southern states seemed ready to oppose the national party or at least use that threat to persuade the national convention to restore the two-thirds majority rule for presidential nominations. Its abolishment in 1936 at Roosevelt's request had removed the veto power the South had over the party's candidates and platform. But the Texas Democratic party created a tribunal headed by Congressman Wright Patman that removed most of the disloyal candidates for electors and replaced them with men favorable to Roosevelt. Other southern leaders fell in line, and the President went on to beat Thomas E. Dewey in the election by a wide margin.

In 1948 the problem recurred in Alabama. The state Supreme Court offered an advisory opinion to the governor in early 1948 on the constitutionality of a state law requiring that presidential electors cast their votes for the nominee of their party's national convention. The Alabama justices held unanimously that the authors of the federal Constitution intended that electors should exercise their own discretion in voting for President. Electors, they pointed out, are elected by popular vote and appointed by the state.

Since a political party does not choose them, it cannot control them. Therefore, the justices concluded, the Alabama law requiring electors to vote for their party's nominee violated the federal Constitution.[9] Neither the name of President Harry S Truman nor electors favoring him were on the 1948 ballot in Alabama, whose electors voted in the electoral college for Dixiecrat Senator J. Strom Thurmond of South Carolina, who was running for President on the States' Rights party ticket. But the voters generally stayed with the Democrats, and Truman won by 49.6 percent of the popular vote and a plurality of more than two million votes. In the electoral college, he received 303 of 535 votes. Although Truman carried Tennessee, one of that state's Democrat-Dixiecrat electors voted for Thurmond. As in 1796 and 1820, this defection did not affect the outcome of the contest.

In 1952 dissident Alabama Democrats were at work again. The Supreme Court on April 15 reversed an Alabama Supreme Court decision and held that the state Democratic chairman could not be required to certify as a candidate for elector in a Democratic primary contest anyone who refused to sign a pledge to support the national party's presidential and vice presidential nominees. Justice Stanley Reed, writing for the Supreme Court majority, indicated that such a loyalty pledge could be required under the authority of the state to regulate elections; nothing in the Constitution would prohibit it. Justices Robert Jackson and William O. Douglas dissented on the grounds that electors have the constitutional right and power to vote for whomever they choose.[10]

Congress seriously considered electoral reform throughout the 1950s. Besides the proportional plan, there was considerable support for the district plan sponsored by Republican Senator Karl Mundt of South Dakota and Republican Representative Frederic R. Coudert of New York. In 1953 the Senate held hearings, and in 1955 its Judiciary Committee reported a proportional plan, spon-

9. Alabama Supreme Court, Opinion of the Justices No. 87, 250 Ala. 399, 34 So. 2d 598 (1948).

10. *Ray* v. *Blair*, 343 U.S. 214 (1952).

sored this time by Democratic Senators Estes Kefauver of Tennessee and Price Daniel of Texas. Opposition to the plan was led by Democratic Senators John F. Kennedy of Massachusetts, who had defeated Senator Lodge in his 1952 bid for reelection, and Paul H. Douglas of Illinois. The plan came to the floor in March 1956. The first tests came on two direct-vote plans. One measure, which included provision for a national presidential primary, lost, 13 to 69; the other, providing only for the direct vote, lost, 17 to 66. The Senate then voted 48 to 37 for a substitute resolution that would have allowed each state to choose between the proportional and the district plans. The majority fell short of the necessary two-thirds of those present and voting.

Later in 1956 the star-crossed relationship between dissident Alabama Democrats and the electoral college was renewed. President Dwight D. Eisenhower defeated Adlai E. Stevenson in the presidential race by a landslide even greater than his 1952 triumph, winning 457 out of 531 electoral votes. In the electoral college, Alabama elector W. F. Turner voted for segregationist Judge Walter B. Jones of his home state for President and Senator Herman E. Talmadge of Georgia for Vice President, in lieu of Stevenson and Kefauver—the Democratic ticket. Turner's was wholly a vote of protest, since there was no way of affecting the overwhelming Eisenhower majority.

The Electoral College in the 1960s

During the past decade two extremely close elections, in which rebel Democrats opposed their national party, have revived old fears that no candidate would win an electoral vote majority. In fact, in both elections the popular winner did receive a majority in the electoral college, but reformers continue to emphasize the theoretical shortcomings of a system that actually has enjoyed marked success.

In 1960 another threat to the electoral college system arose in the South. Although potentially more serious, it was as ineffectual as earlier southern efforts. John F. Kennedy was elected President with 49.5 percent of the popular vote and 303 of the 537 electoral votes.[11] Fourteen electoral votes were cast by unpledged electors from Alabama and Mississippi for Democratic Senators Harry F. Byrd of Virginia for President and Strom Thurmond of South Carolina for Vice President. An additional electoral college vote for Byrd came from Henry D. Irwin, an Oklahoma elector who ran on the Republican ticket. Irwin cast his vice presidential vote for Republican Senator Barry M. Goldwater of Arizona. At Senate hearings in 1961 Irwin testified that he "could not stomach, if you will pardon the expression, voting for Vice President Nixon."[12] He told the senators that through correspondence he had worked with R. Lea Harris, a Montgomery, Alabama, lawyer, whom he said he had never met. They sought to create a Republican-southern Democratic coalition to elect a conservative President in the electoral college. Before the electoral votes were cast, Irwin had wired all the Republican electors and urged them to support his plan. None did. Some senators who heard Irwin's testimony ex-

11. These are the generally accepted figures, and they will be used throughout this study. However, the facts are clouded because in Alabama the names only of electors, not those of the national candidates, appeared on the 1960 ballot; six men on the Democratic slate were unpledged electors who ultimately voted for Senator Byrd, and five were loyalists who cast their electoral ballots for Kennedy. In November many Alabamians voted for some of the unpledged electors and for some of the Kennedy electors. How, then, can the Kennedy popular total be calculated? The usual way is to count as the Kennedy total the popular vote for the Kennedy elector who did best. Similarly, the vote for the leading unpledged elector is counted as the total for the unpledged electors. That system is used in the returns cited above. However, it entails counting twice the popular votes of those Alabamians who voted for some Kennedy electors and some unpledged electors.

An alternative method is to take the highest vote for any Alabama Democratic elector and divide it proportionately among the two groups of electors—six-elevenths to the unpledged group and five-elevenths to the Kennedy forces. Under this system, Kennedy is awarded substantially fewer popular votes in Alabama; in fact, the shift is such that Nixon emerges with a nationwide popular plurality of 58,181.

12. *Nomination and Election of President and Vice President and Qualifications for Voting*, Hearings before the Senate Committee on the Judiciary, 87 Cong. 1 sess. (1961), Pt. 3, p. 644.

pressed shock, but the Senate did not act on electoral reform resolutions. Like other "faithless" electors, Irwin had not significantly changed the election outcome.

On a more philosophical level, during the past ten years the right to vote has been a major—and largely successful—progressive cause. Congress has been a principal arena of the struggle. The Twenty-third Amendment, ratified in 1961, authorized a vote for President and Vice President by District of Columbia residents. The Twenty-fourth Amendment, which was ratified in 1964, banned the poll tax as a voting requirement in federal elections. Civil Rights Acts passed in 1957, 1960, 1964, and 1965 added up to a federal guarantee of the right of all citizens to vote.

The judiciary has also actively promoted the cause of voting rights, notably in a remarkable series of Supreme Court decisions. In a 1962 case the court ruled that a failure to reapportion state legislative districts for fifty years constituted a violation of equal protection of the laws, which is guaranteed by the Fourteenth Amendment.[13] Two years later the court held that the Georgia county unit vote system for aggregating votes in state and congressional primary elections violated the equal protection clause. The court added that defense of the Georgia system on grounds of its similarity to the federal electoral college was an inappropriate analogy. "The concept of political equality," Justice Douglas wrote for the majority, "can only mean one thing—one person, one vote."[14] The next year the court reversed the Georgia Supreme Court and applied the one-person-one-vote standard—this time based on Article I of the Constitution rather than the Fourteenth Amendment—to elections for the national House of Representatives.[15] It reaffirmed its new course in another case with the comment that equal protection of the laws calls for "as nearly . . . equal population as is practicable" for representative purposes.[16]

13. *Baker* v. *Carr*, 369 U.S. 186 (1962).
14. *Gray* v. *Sanders*, 372 U.S. 379 (1964).
15. *Wesberry* v. *Sanders*, 376 U.S. 1 (1965).
16. *Reynolds* v. *Sims*, 377 U.S. 577 (1965).

Despite the obvious broader implications of the one-person-one-vote standard, however, the court has declined to apply it specifically to the electoral college. The state of Delaware, later supported by other states, sued New York and other larger states on the ground that Delaware (like other small states) was denied equal protection of the laws by the general-ticket system now in effect within the electoral college system. The court in 1965 refused without comment to hear the case.[17]

Indeed, despite contentions by direct-vote advocates that the electoral college system is archaic and that their reform plan is another popular voting right whose time has come, there has been vast evolution, but no formal change, in the electoral college since the Twelfth Amendment was ratified in 1804. Despite recurrent attempts by southern extremists to manipulate the electoral college, the winner of the popular vote has invariably triumphed in the twentieth century. Surely inertia and chance alone are not responsible for the persistence and functional effectiveness of the electoral college system. For the substantive factors supporting the existing system, a more detailed examination of its operation and effects is needed.

17. *Delaware* v. *New York*, 385 U.S. 964 (1966).

☆

Chapter Three

☆

THE EXISTING SYSTEM

"Nobody has a kind word for the outmoded electoral college," Robert Bendiner has written, "but only professors and cartoonists get really worked up about it."[1] While that is an exaggeration, it has a certain ring of truth. Most of the words penned and uttered in the electoral college debate have been critical of various effects of the system. And yet the system has its defenders, including Professors Alexander Bickel of the Yale Law School, Irving Kristol of New York University, and many of the nation's political scientists.[2] They believe that the electoral college system operates essentially to buttress the two-party political tradition, the presidential office, the balance of power between metropolitan centers and outlying areas, and the federal structure. Without such a defense, accepted by many political leaders, the system would hardly have survived since 1789.

This chapter will examine the contemporary electoral college: how it functions, its evident political impact, and the underlying issues of political values.

At present, the President is elected under rules set forth by the Constitution and by the federal and state laws and political party rules that carry out its mandate. In November of every fourth year, qualified voters may go to the polls to cast their votes for President. Most of those who are eligible *do* vote, although the turnout is lower than in many other countries. Exactly what they

1. Robert Bendiner, *White House Fever* (Harcourt, Brace & Co., 1960), p. 130.
2. See the bibliography at the end of this book.

may vote for varies from state to state. In thirty-five states, the names of the party's presidential and vice presidential nominees alone are listed on a "short" ballot. In Alabama, only slates of presidential electors chosen by the state party are listed. And in fourteen additional states and certain parts of two short-ballot states the names of both the candidates and the electors who would presumably vote for them in the electoral college are printed on the ballot. Moreover, states like Alabama and Mississippi allow "unpledged" electors to be on the ballot, indicating the state party's opposition to the national ticket and the presumed intention of the state party's electors to vote for other candidates in the electoral college. Nominees for elector are chosen by their state parties in a variety of ways, most commonly (in thirty-five states) at the state convention; they are usually, but not always, lesser party functionaries. Some fifteen states now require by law that electors vote for the presidential slate of their national party; but many legal experts question whether such provisions can be enforced.

In addition, state laws vary regarding the eligibility of parties, notably minor parties, to appear on the ballot. For example, some states have rules for minor parties, some for independent candidacies, some for both. In some states a minor party is automatically put on the ballot if it won a certain percentage of the vote in the previous election; in some, a minor-party or independent candidate may be placed on the ballot on petition of a certain number of qualified voters; in some states a minor party is allowed on the ballot when a specified number of voters have registered as members. The percentages of voters required and the amount of time allowed for the petition and registration procedures also vary from state to state.

In these differing contexts, citizens vote in November, choosing in each state as many electors as the state has senators plus representatives. Including the three to which the District of Columbia is entitled this means a total of 538 electors. In every election since 1920, and with few exceptions since 1836, all of each state's electors have been awarded to the party that received a plurality of that state's popular votes; this is the "winner-take-all" or "general-ticket" system. However, in early 1969 Maine adopted a district plan, under which two electors are chosen on a statewide popular level and one from each of the state's two congressional districts. The only other exceptions since 1920 have been the four electors who individually bolted their tickets, and the unusual situation in Alabama in 1960 (five Democratic electors were loyal to Kennedy; the remaining six on the Democratic slate were "unpledged" but cast their electoral votes for Senator Harry F. Byrd). Members of each winning electoral slate are certified by the governor in a document sent to the federal General Services Administration in Washington.

On the first Monday after the second Wednesday in December, each group of electors meets in its state and formally casts its votes. Generally there is also some kind of ceremony in which state officials take part. Almost without fail, each elector votes for the presidential ticket on which he is running. In American history, only 6 out of 16,510 electors—a mere statistical trace—have not; none has changed the outcome of an election. The electors cast ballots separately for President and Vice President, and the official results are sent to Washington. There they go to the president of the Senate, the incumbent Vice President. After the certificates have been opened and officially counted at a joint session of Congress on January 6, the president of the Senate formally announces the result. The candidate having a majority of the electoral votes for President is elected President, and the candidate with a majority of the votes for Vice President is elected to that office.

However, if no candidates received electoral college majorities, the choice would be made by the Congress that convened January 3. In these circumstances the House, with each state delegation casting one vote, would choose the President from "the persons having the highest numbers not exceeding three on the list of those voted for as President," in the language of the Twelfth Amendment. A quorum for this purpose consists of at least one representative from each of two-thirds of the state delegations. Balloting would continue until one candidate received an absolute majority of all states. If the House could not agree before Inauguration Day, the newly elected Vice President would become acting President. If no one had been elected Vice President by the electoral college, a majority of the Senate would choose from the two candidates highest in electoral college votes for that office.

The Constitution and statutes do not cover what would happen if a candidate for either President or Vice President died between the time his party nominated him and the day the electoral college voted. Every four years, national party conventions pass resolutions to deal with the problem. Usually the Democratic party has empowered the national committee to fill any vacancy, with each state or territory casting as many votes as it did at that year's national convention. The Republican resolution has provided either for the same procedure or for a new convention called by the GOP national committee. The Twenty-fifth Amendment stipulates that if the President-elect should die after the electoral college has balloted, the Vice President-elect would succeed to the presidency; if the Vice President-elect died, the President-elect after he took office would nominate a Vice President to be approved by Congress.

The rules of politics are never neutral; they always help or hurt various contestants for power. Thus, the procedure under which a President is elected has far-flung, often little-noted, and sometimes misunderstood effects on many aspects of the political system, which should be considered in assessing the merits of the electoral college. It is a difficult task to weigh the precise impact of an electoral system, which is only one of a number of factors influencing the political process. We cannot prove an exclusive cause-and-effect relationship. All we can do is to state the logical implications of the electoral system, the behavior that has taken place within it, and the observations of scholars about it. We believe, however, that the political effects of the electoral college system are as clear as any in the nonexact science of American politics.

Metropolitan Orientation

The major metropolitan areas of populous states are the principal presidential constituency under the existing electoral system. The method of allocating electoral votes among the states, like the representation scheme for Congress, was originally intended to balance small-state and large-state interests. Although the principle of the old compromise remains, the political situation has changed. On balance, the populous states are more powerful. They have always been predominant. In the first election, in 1789, some 39 percent of the states—Virginia (12 votes), Massachusetts (10), Pennsylvania (10), Maryland (8), and New York (8)—accounted for more than half of the total of 81 electoral votes. Today the power is still more concentrated. Twenty-four percent of the states—New York (43), California (40), Pennsylvania (29), Illinois (26), Ohio (26), Texas (25), Michigan (21), New Jersey (17), Massachusetts (14), Florida (14), and North Carolina (13) —account for just under half of the 538 electoral votes. Moreover, the gap between large and small states is greater today. In 1789 the largest state, Virginia, had 12 votes; the smallest state, Delaware, had 3. In 1968 the largest state, New York, had 43 votes; the smallest state, Alaska, still had only 3. Finally, and most important, the general-ticket system has worked to the advantage of the populous states. In 1789, when states chose electors in a variety of ways, theoretically not all of a state's electors had to go to the statewide winner. In 1968 every state operated under the general-ticket system, which makes populous states the focus of presidential campaigns.

Yet the power of populous states in determining the outcome of presidential elections should not be overstated. The American electorate, like American society generally, has become greatly nationalized in the twentieth century. The mass communications media, in particular, have done much to blur state lines. This means that the large state–small state distinction is less important than is often believed. The power of populous states would be overwhelming if they were able to exercise their will in presidential elections over the opposition of smaller states—that is, if their votes were consolidated to elect a President who was opposed by the other states. There is no evidence that this is the case.

Instead, voting in populous states appears to reflect opinion in the country as a whole. When the country is divided, the populous states are divided also. Thus, in 1960 John F. Kennedy won eight of the eleven largest states, by popular pluralities ranging from 50.0 percent in Illinois to 60.2 percent in Massachusetts; Richard M. Nixon won three of the most populous states, with pluralities from 50.1 percent in California to 53.3 percent in Ohio. Again, in 1968 Nixon carried six of these states with pluralities from 39.5 percent in North Carolina to 47.8 percent in California; Hubert H. Humphrey carried the remaining five states with pluralities ranging from 41.1 percent in Texas to 63.0 percent in Massachusetts. Similarly, when the nation produces a landslide, so do the large states. In 1964 Lyndon B. Johnson carried every one of the eleven most populous states by pluralities ranging from 51.1 percent in Florida to 76.2 percent in Massachusetts. In the eleven states studied, the median plurality for a statewide presidential winner was 51.1 percent in the close two-way race in 1960 and 47.1 percent in the three-way 1968 race; the median was 63.3 percent in the one-sided contest of 1964.

More important politically, under the existing electoral system major metropolitan areas cast the lion's share of the populous states' votes. As a result the cities and their large blocs of voters are of great consequence in presidential elections. This phenomenon is fully recognized in the conventional wisdom of American politics.

Perhaps less well known is that suburbs, as distinct from the core-city areas of populous states, also have important voting power under the present system. Suburbs, of course, are associated with cities as elements in the metropolitan centers that contribute to the voting power of populous states. Although suburbanites have not tended to vote as heavily in one direction as certain core-city groups have, they have done so on occasion. In heterogeneous states like Ohio that went for Richard Nixon by a narrow margin in 1968, the suburbs, while not monolithic, were probably decisive.

Rural and small town areas are at a relative disadvantage under the present electoral college scheme, and their disadvantage will continue so long as they are less populous than the metropolitan areas. It will be particularly acute so long as the major states are dominated by metropolitan areas and cast their electoral votes under the general-ticket system.

The metropolitan swing-vote effect is often interpreted to mean that Negroes and other ethnic groups concentrated in the major urban areas are powerful beyond their numbers in presidential elections. Many political leaders, including some presidential candidates, have accepted this interpretation. Some supporters of the Lodge-Gossett amendment during the 1950s had this phenomenon in mind in seeking to end the general-ticket system. The problem with a swing-vote theory, however, is that any one of a number of voting groups can be identified as crucial. In making this point during the 1956 Senate electoral reform debate, the then-junior senator from Massachusetts, John F. Kennedy, said:

> Several years ago in Fall River, Massachusetts, the mayor was elected by a margin of one vote. That is a very terrible thing to have happen to any politician, because then everyone can say to him: "I elected you."[3]

Similarly, suburbs as well as core-city areas can provide the votes to swing a state from one column to another; and suburban electorates are growing more rapidly than are central city electorates.

The importance of populous states, their major metropolitan areas, and their large blocs of ethnic groups has tended to make presidential candidates "liberal" in domestic policy, sensitive to urban ethnic group concerns in both domestic and foreign policy, and "internationalist" in foreign policy—or at least more so than they otherwise would be. Presidential candidates have stressed these areas in their campaigns, and political scientists writing

3. *Congressional Record*, Vol. 102, Pt. 4, 84 Cong. 2 sess. (1956), p. 5250.

about such contests have invariably taken note of this pattern.[4]
Core cities have wanted the federal government services advocated
by liberals in education, welfare programs, housing, and the like.
To appeal to voters seeking these services, presidential candidates
at least had to appear to be well disposed toward such programs.
Again, because Negroes, Puerto Ricans, Mexican-Americans,
Jews, Poles, Italians, Irishmen, and so on have comprised important voting blocs, presidential candidates have had to give attention to issues that concern them. Thus, for Negroes and others
it has been civil rights, jobs, and welfare; for Jews it has been
Israel, anti-Semitism, and various social reform measures. Other
groups have had similar concerns but have been less influential.
Finally, since the coastal areas of the United States—generally
synonymous with major metropolitan areas—tend to be more internationalist than the midlands, presidential candidates in seeking
votes in these areas have had reason to be internationalist. Of
course, being "internationalist" provides only the most general
sort of policy direction; broadly speaking, in the postwar era
internationalism has meant support for U.S. foreign aid and for
the United Nations. There has been sharp division over such military involvement as that in Southeast Asia.

All this should not be taken to mean that the existing electoral
system assures a liberal, internationalist President. For one thing,
building a majority of electoral votes requires support in states
other than those dominated by metropolitan areas. Traditionally,
the Democrats have looked to the South and the Republicans to
the Midwest and upper New England for additional votes—areas
where the two parties have had great strength. Now that these sections are becoming less attached to one or another of the major
parties than they were in the past, this pattern is changing. But the
principle that the metropolitan areas are not the only constituency
of the President still obtains. Moreover, there is no assurance that
the views of all groups in metropolitan areas will always be liberal

4. See, for example, Nelson W. Polsby and Aaron B. Wildavsky, *Presidential Elections* (2nd ed., Scribners, 1968), pp. 31–33.

or internationalist. Ethnic groups that were "liberal" in the 1930s, when the term meant to them support for broad federal government social welfare measures, are not necessarily "liberal" in the 1970s, when the word to them implies preferential treatment for blacks and little emphasis on law and order. The issues have changed. The ethnic groups themselves may also have changed; many of the group members may now have a greater stake in the existing order and may be less willing to support change, and the younger ones may identify less with the group, especially in political matters.[5] Similarly, the meaning of "internationalism" has changed; support for U.S. intervention abroad has probably lessened in the metropolitan areas from the immediate postwar period to the era of involvement in Southeast Asia. Thus, the predominant views and even the balance of power may shift within the large metropolitan areas; but in any case they have important leverage in presidential elections that they would not have without the general-ticket electoral-vote system.

The Political Party System

The existing electoral college system, in our opinion, encourages a two-party system. When trying to explain the two-party phenomenon, political scientists—perhaps oriented toward parliamentary systems—have usually focused on the national legislative body. A country that has single-member legislative districts instead of proportional representation, scholars have argued, is likely to have two major political parties. Thus, where legislative seats are not allocated by fractions of the nationwide vote but by geographic units on a winner-take-all basis, smaller parties destined for failure either give up or resign themselves to impotence. Much the same is true of the presidential electoral system. One Chief Executive is elected; and he is elected by a majority of electoral

5. On the persistence of ethnic voting patterns, see Raymond E. Wolfinger, "The Development and Persistence of Ethnic Voting," *American Political Science Review*, Vol. 59 (December 1965), pp. 896–908.

votes cast under the state general-ticket system, not by a proportional vote-counting procedure. Surely the electoral college system is even more conducive to two parties than is the congressional election system; it would be easier for a minor party to carry a few congressional districts than a few states. The electoral college system is doubly important because the presidency is the richest prize in American politics.

The historical record suggests the two-party bias. Since the Civil War, minor party candidates have won electoral votes in only five presidential contests. In 1892 the Populists received 22 electoral votes; in 1912 the Roosevelt Progressives received 88 votes; in 1924 the LaFollette Progressives won 13 votes; in 1948 the Thurmond States' Rights party received 39 votes; and in 1968 the George Wallace ticket won 46 electoral votes. The highest popular vote percentage achieved by a minor party candidate during this period was Theodore Roosevelt's 27.4 percent in 1912. James B. Weaver received 8.5 percent in 1892; LaFollette, 16.6 percent in 1924; Thurmond, 2.4 percent in 1948; and George Wallace, 13.5 percent in 1968.

Although minor parties have made important contributions to American political life, only those that are strong within a particular state or region can have an impact on electoral outcomes; only those with a chance of carrying some states' electoral votes have any hope of directly affecting the presidential race. As Alexander Heard has written, "Third parties in America are doomed so long as our present constitutional arrangements are maintained."[6] Minor parties with an effective sectional base have sometimes amassed electoral votes and, in states like New York, have tipped the balance between the major parties. Consequently, if the leaders of minor parties calculate rationally, either they endorse the major party slate they prefer or, acting as "spoilers" attempting to defeat a major party, they run their own slate. The only logical reason for deviating from this pattern is pressure from

6. Alexander Heard, *A Two-Party South?* (University of North Carolina Press, 1952), p. 31.

rank and file party members to mount a separate slate, but this rarely occurs.

As an alternative to a minor party acting as a "spoiler" on the state level, it will be recalled, southern dissidents in 1960 tried to manipulate the election outcome through their control over the choice of candidates for elector. Mississippi Democratic leaders, unwilling to accept John F. Kennedy and his platform, put up and elected a slate of electors who were labeled "unpledged" but were overtly hostile to the national party ticket. They voted for Senator Harry F. Byrd of Virginia in the electoral college. Six unpledged electors on a mixed Alabama Democratic slate did the same. The effect of their maneuvers was little more than to register a well publicized protest. Unpledged Alabama Democratic electors lost to Barry Goldwater's Republican slate in 1964. Efforts to elect unpledged electors have since been abandoned, probably permanently.

When a large, pluralistic society like the United States has a two-party system in which minor parties are effective only at the fringes, the major parties are inevitably heterogeneous. Each contains a variety of social and economic strata, ethnic groups, religions, ideological factions, and sectional groups. And despite the preeminence of populous states in presidential elections, few candidates dare direct their campaigns to those states alone. Furthermore, political parties are concerned with more than the presidency; there are also gubernatorial, Senate, and House seats to be won, plus a plethora of other state and local offices.

The parties are heterogeneous not only in composition but in ideology as well. Republican presidential contenders in 1968 ranged from Ronald Reagan to Nelson Rockefeller; the Democratic party of Eugene J. McCarthy until recently included George Wallace. American parties simply do not fit the responsible party government model favored by many liberal and conservative ideologues. The state electoral vote system encourages philosophical pluralism. A Republican candidate like Richard Nixon seeks to win votes of Negroes in populous-state slums by espousing "black capitalism"; he reminds whites in smaller states that he supports capitalism, and law and order as well. Hubert Humphrey, the South's choice among available Democrats in 1968, reminds blacks of his twenty years of leadership in the civil rights cause. Such appeals are born of the necessity to develop a national constituency. While that principle would remain the same, strategic and tactical concerns might be different under alternative electoral arrangements; this issue is discussed in later chapters of this book.

PARTY ORGANIZATION AND COMPETITION

The electoral vote system has also affected the nature of party organization. The system gives the states strategic political importance. Because a presidential victory is won by putting together blocs of state electoral votes, there is great stress among political leaders on "carrying" California, New York, Ohio, and other large competitive states. Winning groups of states, rather than winning a majority or plurality of the voters nationwide, is the objective of the enterprise. Accordingly, state leaders are important to those engaged in a presidential campaign. The same is true of powerful local leaders, particularly those from major metropolitan areas. Since there is no political reason for strong national organizations, there are none, other than ephemeral campaign organizations. The formal national party committees are hyperactive in coordinating activities every four years and relatively passive during intervening periods, as are other national citizens' groups established in election campaigns for fund-raising and for appeals to specific nationwide constituencies. Indeed, the national committees consist primarily of state and local party leaders.

Contrary to some assertions, the effect of the electoral college system on party competition within states is slight. Some Republicans and others have argued that the state general-ticket system encourages one-party areas. In the South, they have contended, the GOP had little incentive to mount a major presidential campaign; local Republicans realized that the Democrats would get more popular votes and hence all the state's electoral votes, so why bother? It has also been argued that Democrats did much the same in rock-ribbed Republican states. Common sense supports such a view; and historically the minority party in one-party states often behaved in this way. But times have changed. The number of one-party areas has declined for a variety of reasons—greater mobility of the population, the influence of television, greater aggressiveness of minority parties, some important political conversions, and so on. Today, without any change in the electoral system, a Republican presidential candidate has as good a chance in the South as a Democrat does, other things being equal; a strong Democratic presidential candidate can carry New England and middle western states that were once Republican strongholds.

The electoral vote system has had a definite influence on the nominating process. During the twentieth century the nominee for President—and sometimes the one for Vice President—has tended to come from a populous, doubtful state. Party leaders presume that the candidate can carry his home state and that if he appeals to voters in one large state, he will appeal to voters in others. Consider some recent Republican and Democratic nominees: Thomas E. Dewey of New York, Adlai E. Stevenson of Illinois, Richard M. Nixon of California (who was a resident of New York when he was nominated in 1968), John F. Kennedy of Massachusetts, and Lyndon B. Johnson of Texas. Indeed, plaintiffs in the *Delaware* v. *New York* case[7] listed among their grievances the unlikelihood that a Delaware resident would ever be nominated for President under the existing electoral scheme. Of the thirty-six nominations made by major parties from 1900 to 1968, fourteen went to candidates from New York. With the nationalization of campaigns, however, particularly through the use of network television, the tendency to nominate a candidate from a populous state may have become less pronounced. This trend may help explain the selection of Barry M. Goldwater, Hubert H. Humphrey, Edmund S. Mus-

7. 385 U.S. 964 (1966).

kie, and Spiro T. Agnew. Other factors were apparently more decisive in these instances.

Campaigns have similarly tended to concentrate on populous states and their metropolitan areas. Political strategists go where the most votes are to be won. Usually this means focusing on densely populated areas whose turnout rate and/or choice is doubtful. For Democrats this means giving prime attention to New York City, Philadelphia, Chicago, Los Angeles, and so on; in a close race these major cities may swing a state's entire bloc of electoral votes. Some Republicans also follow a similar pattern, though they concentrate on the suburbs rather than the central cities. But there are other strategies. Richard Nixon visited all fifty states in 1960 (and, having lost, adopted a different strategy in 1968). Barry Goldwater in 1964 apparently sought to capture almost everything but the core cities of major metropolitan areas; his statewide victories came in the deep South and in his native Arizona. In 1968 Nixon reportedly aimed at winning several large states, the "Republican" states of upper New England, many southern and midwestern states, and most of the Far West; he was essentially successful. The policies and appeals of the candidate are of crucial importance. True, most winning campaigns since New Deal days have focused primarily on big cities; that has seemed the most efficient way for a Democrat to win, and generally Democrats have won since 1932. But there are other ways of accumulating electoral votes totaling 270 or more.

Does the existing electoral system have particular significance for voters and their behavior? It has some significance perhaps but probably less than critics have contended. Traditionally, metropolitan area voters in populous states have received more attention in campaigns because their votes have been strategically more important. Whatever the finer calculations, it has been quite reasonable to assume that New Yorkers would have a greater opportunity to see presidential candidates in person than would their fellow countrymen living in Velva, North Dakota. Some critics have charged that such uneven exposure encourages apathy among the voters of the "less important" states. We doubt it. Much of the South, for example, became an important battleground in 1968 as three candidates vigorously sought its support. Again, presidential primary contests in relatively obscure states like New Hampshire or West Virginia may give them critical importance during the course of a campaign. And still more important, increasing reliance on national television has meant that all voters have an opportunity to familiarize themselves with presidential candidates. Thus, campaigning has become more nearly uniform throughout the country. Finally, voter apathy is a product of many forces besides a lack of campaigning in the voter's locality. Nonvoters, for example, tend to be those with the least education and the lowest socioeconomic status. Campaigning produces only a limited stimulus to voter interest.

The electoral college system probably has no effect on voter choices. Survey research on electoral behavior has established that voters' decisions are based on their attitudes toward the parties, the candidates, and salient issues. Although they register their preferences through a slate of electors, and although some might occasionally cast a ballot for a personal acquaintance or respected figure running for elector, voters generally are motivated by the underlying factors. They perceive the election as a national contest.

A PARTISAN BIAS?

Does the present electoral system tend to help Democrats or Republicans? And which faction of each party does it favor? Republicans and others often claim that the existing system, because of its metropolitan bias, inherently favors Democrats. However, it was pointed out above that populous states usually divide their votes between the parties about as the country as a whole does and that over the years party leaders themselves have adopted various strategies in addition to concentrating on metropolitan areas in order to win. Dwight D. Eisenhower had little difficulty in winning the presidency twice by decisive margins; Richard M. Nixon, who benefited from a popular issue-orientation in his direction, was also able to muster the requisite votes. Any difficulty Republicans face in winning presidential elections begins with the fact that there are fewer self-identified Republicans than Democrats in the electorate, rather than that popular votes are tallied by states.

On the other hand, a few observers have contended that the electoral vote system is biased in favor of the Republicans. For example, Louis H. Bean noted that during the period 1916–36 the Democrats won only when they received at least 53 percent of the two-party vote.[8] Others have pointed out that since the Republicans began nominating presidential candidates in 1856, they have usually won close contests in which no candidate captured a majority of the popular vote. Here again, there is no conclusive trend. Since the period studied by Bean, Democrats have twice won with less than 53 percent of the two-party vote: Harry S Truman received 52.4 percent in 1948, and John F. Kennedy got slightly over 50 percent, at best,[9] of the popular votes cast for Nixon and Kennedy in 1960. Since 1936 the Republicans have won one close election—in 1968. Since 1856 the record of victories without a popular majority is mixed: Republicans won five times under those circumstances, in 1860, 1876, 1880, 1888, and 1968; Democrats won seven times, in 1856, 1884, 1892, 1912, 1916, 1948, and 1960. The existing electoral vote system does not seem to have helped either party substantially.

Does the system have a significant impact on intraparty politics? Generally, the northern, coastal, urban wing has had a decisive influence on presidential nominations of the Democratic party since southern influence began to decline with the end in 1936 of the rule requiring a majority of two-thirds for nomination at the Democratic national convention. The Republican picture is more cloudy. Nominees have ranged from Alfred M. Landon and

8. Louis H. Bean, *Ballot Behavior* (Public Affairs Press, 1961), pp. 40–41.

9. If Kennedy is credited with the votes won by the highest Alabama elector pledged to him, he emerges with 50.08 percent of the two-party vote (49.5 percent of the total presidential vote). On the problem of counting the Alabama vote, see Chap. 2.

Wendell Willkie to Barry M. Goldwater. Conservative Republicans long charged that conventions were rigged in favor of an "East-Coast Establishment" that produced such candidates as Thomas E. Dewey and Dwight D. Eisenhower. Yet conservatives easily succeeded in nominating Goldwater in 1964; and Richard Nixon in 1968 was not an Establishment candidate either. These patterns suggest that the outcome of internal party struggles is determined essentially by factors other than the allocation of electoral college votes. Logically those factors include the location of partisans within the country and the strategic choices of the parties' leaders. Outside the South, Democrats tend to be strongest in the cities of populous states. They have won many presidential elections by concentrating on those areas, and quite sensibly they tend to repeat the successful pattern; accordingly political leaders from the strong areas are influential within the party. Republicans tend to have more support outside the cities; but since 1932 they have lost the presidency more frequently than they have won it. As a result, the Republican campaign focus has vacillated between areas where they have been strongest traditionally and areas where Democrats have been successful.

The Presidency

One obvious but frequently overlooked political effect of the electoral college system is that it has always produced a President and a Vice President. It has generally done so—particularly during the period of Democratic-Republican two-party dominance—without prolonged indecision; and because of a strong two-party norm, combined with the state general-ticket system, there has been no need to resort to a contingency election since 1836. Since only rarely do third parties capture electoral votes, it is virtually certain that one of the major parties will obtain an electoral college majority.

The successful functioning of the electoral college system has fostered political stability for the U.S. government. The results of presidential elections, and the extent to which the American people accept the results, directly affect the presidency as an institution and the larger system of which it is a part. In later chapters we shall discuss whether alternative electoral arrangements seem conducive to comparable stability.

The orderly way in which a President has always been elected has meant less political unrest than is found in many other countries. Demagoguery among presidential contenders has been rare and has been confined to minor parties or candidates who have no chance to win. In U.S. history there have been few of the riots that have taken place in many developing nations during elections. There have been none of the street gangs and party armies that there were in Weimar Germany. There have not been constant cabinet crises as in pre- (and probably post-) Gaullist France. There have been no military coups. Americans must not be too smug about the peacefulness of their elections, however, lest they gloss over a few assassinations, a few governors with personal police forces, and Negro "citizens" long disfranchised. But the relative calm with which most Americans have accepted the outcome of the electoral process every four years was symbolized by a brief, gracious speech given by Richard M. Nixon. In 1961, when, as president of the Senate, he supervised the counting of the electoral votes and announced his own defeat and the victory of John F. Kennedy, Nixon said:[10]

> I do not think we could have a more striking and eloquent example of the stability of our Constitutional system and of the proud tradition of the American people of developing, respecting, and honoring institutions of self-government.
>
> In our campaigns, no matter how hard fought they may be, no matter how close the election may turn out to be, those who lose accept the verdict and support those who win.

The electoral system also encourages political moderation. It supports a system in which two broadly based, heterogeneous political parties compete for the votes of the electorate. Minor parties

10. *Congressional Record*, Vol. 107, Pt. 1 (1961), p. 291.

attract far fewer voters, not nearly enough to elect a President, and only rarely enough to elect even a congressman. The non-ideological politics enjoyed by the United States differs, for example, from politics in France and Italy, where political divisions are many and more sharply drawn.

Under the electoral college system, the President has usually been elected with a majority of the popular votes. However, a President has sometimes been elected without a popular majority, or (much more rarely) without even a popular plurality. Fifteen times out of thirty-seven, the winner has not received a majority of the popular vote: in 1824 (when the popular vote count was first available but was incomplete because in six states there was no popular vote for President), 1844, 1848, 1856, 1860, 1876, 1880, 1884, 1888, 1892, 1912, 1916, 1948, 1960, and 1968. Three times —in 1824, 1876, and 1888—the winner officially had fewer popular votes than his principal opponent. In 1824 the popular vote was not national. If in 1876 Samuel Tilden, the popular vote winner, had received the southern electoral votes to which he may well have been entitled, he would have won. In 1888, as in 1824 and 1876, no candidate received a popular majority; less than 100,000 popular votes separated the two key contenders in 1888.

How likely is it that the winner of a popular plurality could lose in electoral college votes? One measure of the probability is the historical record. No winner of a plurality has lost a presidential election in the twentieth century. To put it another way, in the twenty most recent presidential elections—over a period of eighty years—the plurality winner has always won an electoral college majority.

There is another way to measure the likelihood of such an occurrence. A "runner-up President" could theoretically be elected by rolling up large popular pluralities in some states and losing narrowly in others that had large blocs of electoral votes. That is what happened in 1888. That year, when one-party states still were a potent force and were strongly oriented toward the Democrats, Grover Cleveland did extremely well in the South. At the same time, however, Benjamin Harrison carried eight of the eleven most populous states—all of them except Missouri, Kentucky, and Texas, and many by narrow margins—and with them put together a victory in electoral votes.

The importance of the most populous states in presidential elections has not changed greatly since 1888; the decline in one-party states has made it far less likely that the runner-up in popular votes will be elected President. The number of states accounting for a majority of the electoral votes has not changed substantially: In 1880 thirteen states had a total of 59.1 percent of the electoral votes; in 1884 and 1888 eleven states had 51.9 percent; in 1960 twelve states represented 51.6 percent; and in 1964 and 1968 twelve states controlled 52.2 percent of the electoral votes. In each of the six years, and with little difference between the two decades, this same group of populous states accounted for 60 percent or more of the popular votes. Finally, in each year except 1884 a majority of the populous states were carried by the party that won the election; and in each year except 1884 a majority of the electoral votes of the populous states was won by the party that won the election. In 1884 the electoral and popular votes of the South were nonetheless enough for Grover Cleveland to win despite James G. Blaine's showing in the major states; in 1888 popular votes from the South gave Cleveland a popular plurality, but Harrison's showing in the major states was decisive in denying Cleveland reelection.

One-party states are thus the major contributors to any discrepancy between the results of the popular vote and those of the electoral vote. The more one-party states and the more electoral and popular votes they have, the greater their impact on the election and the greater the possibility of divergence between the popular and the electoral vote.

Today, this threat is remote. One-party states were far less significant in the presidential elections of the 1960s than they were in the 1880s, when the last (and perhaps only) runner-up President was elected. ("One-party states" are defined here as those in

which a single party won 55 percent or more of the popular vote
for President.) In 1880 there were sixteen one-party states—42
percent of all states; in 1884 there were also sixteen, or 42 percent;
in 1888 there were thirteen one-party states, or 34 percent. In
1960 there were twelve one-party states, only 24 percent of all
states. In 1968 there were the same number and percentage. In the
landslide year 1964, forty-two states and the District of Columbia
were carried by a plurality of 55 percent or more; this is so large a
number (84.3 percent of all states), essentially skewed in a single
direction, that it is clearly a deviant case.

One-party states during the 1960s also accounted for a smaller
percentage of the total electoral vote than during the 1880s. In
1880 one-party states constituted 34.4 percent of the electoral
vote; in 1884 some 30.4 percent; in 1888, 23.2 percent. In 1960
one-party states represented only 16.8 percent of the electoral
vote total, and in 1968, only 12.1 percent.

In the aggregate, the one-party states' electoral college votes in
the 1960s were less biased toward a single party than in the 1880s.
(Net bias is figured here by subtracting the total electoral college
votes in the one-party states won by the party with fewer such
votes from those won by the party with more.) In 1880 there was
a net Democratic bias of 35 electoral college votes; in 1884, a net
Democratic bias of 36 electoral college votes; in 1888, a net Democratic bias of 43 electoral college votes. In 1960 there was a net
Republican bias of 4 electoral college votes, and in 1968 a net
Democratic bias of 8 electoral college votes (if one-party states
going to George Wallace are excluded).

The popular votes of one-party states also accounted for a
smaller percentage of total popular votes during the 1960s than
during the 1880s. In 1880 these states cast 17.6 percent of the
popular vote; in 1884, 13.4 percent; in 1888, 9.7 percent. In 1960
one-party states cast 8.3 percent of the popular total, and in 1968,
only 5.8 percent. Popular votes from one-party states also accounted for less of each major party's popular total during the
1960s than during the 1880s. For the Democrats, in 1880 the pop-

ular votes from one-party states amounted to 21.2 percent of their nationwide popular total; in 1884 they represented 18.0 percent; in 1888, 13.4 percent. In 1960 these votes constituted 7.4 percent of the party total, and in 1968, 7.1 percent. For the Republicans, in 1880 one-party votes accounted for 15.3 percent of the party total nationwide; in 1884, 9.9 percent, and in 1888, 6.6 percent. In 1960 they were 9.4 percent, and in 1968, only 2.9 percent.

It is obvious from this analysis that one-party states are on the wane by any measure, and that consequently there is a declining likelihood of runner-up Presidents. The trend seems unlikely to change unless the kind of one-party sectionalism that developed after the Civil War returns as a potent force in American political life. However, it seems likely to us that the present trend toward the nationalization of politics will continue, and even accelerate, if other factors are constant.

Indeed, rather than producing runner-up Presidents, the present system tends to increase the popular vote winner's margin in the electoral college. This is because under the general-ticket system the states cast their votes as units; and thus each populous state, no matter how closely divided, contributes all its large bloc of votes to the winner of its popular vote. The result is that in 1960, for example, John F. Kennedy captured a nationwide popular plurality of only about 112,000 votes but defeated Richard M. Nixon in the electoral college by a count of 303 to 219. The 1968 outcome was similar; Nixon won 43 percent of the popular votes but 56 percent of the electoral votes. This bias gives the popular plurality winner a decisive victory. He does not have to go through a runoff to be elected. And even if he wins only a plurality of the popular votes, he has won that symbol of legitimacy—a majority of the electoral votes. Having a strong popular mandate—or even the appearance of such strength—is an important base of presidential power. We believe that a President elected under the existing system takes office well equipped to govern because of this firm electoral base.

Many critics of the electoral college system do not believe that it assures election of a President with a solid mandate to govern. Most emphasize the possibility of a runner-up President; we have explained why we find that possibility extremely unlikely. Other critics, however, argue that any majority produced in electoral votes is really irrelevant to the voters and political leaders, who judge the President's mandate by his showing in the popular vote. Perhaps that is in fact the basis of their judgment. But it must be remembered that the existing system has discouraged minor parties and as a result has produced Presidents with either a popular majority (in twenty-two of the thirty-seven contests during the era of nationwide popular returns, from 1824 to the present) or a popular plurality (twelve times), the only three exceptions being in 1824, 1876, and 1888, for reasons already discussed. Thirty-three of the thirty-seven Presidents elected received at least 45 percent of the popular vote. Abraham Lincoln in the unusual election of 1860 was lowest, with 39.8 percent. Even from the standpoint of the popular vote, then, the Presidents chosen under the present system have almost invariably had a solid popular mandate.

We believe that the electoral vote system serves as an additional source of strength for the President taking office. It provides him with a broad base of support. He must produce a coalition of states with wide and diverse interests. He must appeal to a variety of voters for a variety of reasons. He cannot win on the labor vote alone, or the law-and-order vote alone, or an economic protest vote alone, as he conceivably could if only the popular vote were counted and the number of parties increased (see Chapter 4). In some contests, the electoral vote system adds a further dimension of legitimacy to the popular vote mandate. Moreover, electoral votes are not irrelevant to political reality. They are awarded to the states, just as seats in Congress are awarded to the states, after each decennial census, on the basis of a minimum of three for each state with additional votes based on state population. This system does not reflect the popular vote exactly, but it is not intended to; it is a reasonable basis for allocating votes within a federal system of government. If it seemed inclined to produce election winners other than the popular plurality winners, we would find it objectionable despite its virtue of providing a majority coalition. Since the historical record indicates to us that a runner-up President is extremely unlikely, however, we find the assets of the electoral vote system to outweigh its alleged defects.

What about the strength of the presidency as an operating institution? The Constitution established a government of "separate institutions sharing powers"[11]—national and state governments, with the national government composed of legislative, executive, and judicial bodies. Within the national government, the principal institutional tension occurs between the President and Congress. The electoral college gives the President a constituency base different from, and independent of, that of Congress. As V. O. Key, Jr., has written: "The basic arrangement that puts teeth into the system of separated powers is the independent election of President, of Senate, and of House of Representatives."[12] This tends to strengthen the presidency; certainly it is stronger today than it would have been had the founding fathers decided to accept the proposal, put forward by some of their number, that Congress be empowered to choose the President. Once the electoral college has elected him, the President is in office and in power for four years unless he becomes mentally or physically incapacitated, is impeached, or dies. And even if he dies, his elected Vice President assumes office without any intervention by Congress.

Federalism

Aggregating the national popular vote by states under the electoral college system facilitates the working of American federalism. The system represents a compromise between national and state power.

11. Richard E. Neustadt, *Presidential Power* (John Wiley & Sons, 1960), p. 33.
12. V. O. Key, Jr., *Politics, Parties and Pressure Groups* (5th ed., Thomas Y. Crowell, 1964), p. 572.

While there is no separate popular vote mandate for the President, the national principle is at work in a more fundamental sense. The President is not chosen on a one-state-one-vote basis. Although each state has two electoral college votes corresponding to its representation in the Senate, it has additional votes by virtue of its representation in the House and thus of its population.

Aggregating the votes by states also means that individual states have certain responsibilities. For example, they determine the way in which their electors are chosen. At present, all except Maine use the general-ticket system; and it is unlikely that any will change unless most others do, since the winner-take-all procedure insures state party leaders the largest possible group of votes. Many political leaders in small states view the general ticket as serving their interests, because with two electors based on their equal representation in the Senate, they have a greater percentage of the electoral college vote than of the popular vote. And many political leaders in populous states believe that the system serves *their* interests because of their large blocs of electoral college votes.

The states also control the administration of elections, except for certain federal voting requirements, principally voting rights for qualified women and Negroes. Each state determines who appears on its ballot; this power is sometimes significant. In 1948 and 1964, for example, citizens in Alabama could vote for Republican electors, or they could vote for Democratic electors who later did not vote in the electoral college for Presidents Truman or Johnson—the Democratic nominees in those years; there was no way for an Alabama voter to cast his ballot for the national Democratic ticket. In Ohio in 1968 it took a ruling of the U.S. Supreme Court to get George Wallace's party on the ballot, by striking down state requirements that the party had not fulfilled.

Remote Contingencies

Critics of the electoral college system have emphasized the ways in which it could fail to work as intended. The likelihood of a runner-up President, the most prominent example of this kind of speculation, deserves serious analysis. Other potential calamities that are frequently anticipated, however, should be dismissed as highly unlikely or virtually irrelevant.

For instance, it is remotely possible that no one would win a majority of the electoral college and that the contest might be thrown into the House, where the candidate with the most electoral votes would lose. In the nonparty contest in 1824 Andrew Jackson, with 99 electoral votes, lost in the House to John Quincy Adams, who had 84. Today one party usually wins both the presidency and a majority in the House. Given this pattern and the rarity of any contingency election, the chances of such a defeat for the front-runner are scant.

It is also remotely conceivable that under the present system there might be a long period when the outcome of an election was in doubt. If the choice went to Congress, quick agreement might be difficult. But the two experiences with this procedure since passage of the Twelfth Amendment suggest that this would not happen. In 1825 John Quincy Adams was elected President on the first ballot in the House, and in 1837 Richard M. Johnson was chosen Vice President on the first ballot in the Senate. For more than 130 years, contingency election by Congress has not been needed.

Again, because of possibly independent-minded electors and congressmen, election of a President and a Vice President from different parties could theoretically occur. But it never has happened since passage of the Twelfth Amendment, which provided for counting the votes for President and Vice President separately and thus precluding the runner-up presidential candidate from being automatically elected his opponent's Vice President. Party loyalty, custom, and the unlikelihood of a contingency election are additional reasons for the success of the presidential ticket system.

Critics of the present system cite the possible impact on a state's entire bloc of electoral votes of factors like bad weather and fraudulent administration of elections. These are simply not of enough consequence to be seriously considered in policy making. They are very rare phenomena of remotely possible significance under any system and, except for the chicanery in 1876, have evidently had little real impact. Critics also express great concern about the absence of federal law to cover the death of an elector or of a candidate before the electoral college casts its votes. State laws and official ingenuity have dealt with the problem as far as electors are concerned. The more serious issue of a vacancy on the ticket is met by resolutions passed by the political parties at their national conventions.

Underlying Controversies

Up to now we have not dealt directly with the fundamental controversies underlying the electoral college debate. The way the electoral college works is a matter of fact. Its exact effects on the political system are more speculative, but still relatively clear. The basic disagreements in the debate stem from varying assessments of those effects and the kind of constituency it is thought the President should have.

Judgments differ sharply about the desirability of the principal political effects of the electoral college system. Advocates of the existing system approve of the power it gives to populous states, their major metropolitan areas, and their minority groups in presidential elections. The political and policy orientations of the existing system obviously arouse strong passions, both pro and con. This is understandable; fundamental political power is at stake. Some more detached observers favor the orientation of the existing electoral college because they believe that metropolitan forces are disproportionately weak elsewhere within the political system. Critics reply that the extra leverage for metropolitan areas is unjustified and that two wrongs do not make a right.

Most of the popular discussion, though considerably less of the scholarly controversy, concerns the effects of the electoral college on the political party system. Some critics, preoccupied with the George Wallace phenomenon, find fault with the leverage the electoral college allows to sectional minor parties and unpledged electors. Defenders believe that the electoral college system permits dissent, sectional or otherwise, without generating real disruption; they emphasize that the system in fact strengthens the major parties.

The desirability of the effects of the existing system on the presidency as an institution is also a matter of great dispute. Supporters of the present system believe that aggregating the vote by states gives popular plurality winners a more decisive victory and encourages political stability. Most critics believe that the popular vote alone should elect the President, and they are unwilling to risk the possibility, however remote, that the plurality winner might lose. Again, advocates of the existing system consider it desirable that the President have an electoral base quite different from that of Congress. Proponents of the district plan, on the other hand, believe that the President and Congress should have the same sort of constituency—meaning the kind of constituency Congress now has. Similarly, defenders of the present system find it reasonable that Congress, a body presumably knowledgeable about the abilities of the candidates, would elect the President and Vice President if the electoral college did not produce a majority. Critics are unhappy with this provision, particularly with the provision that the House would vote by state delegations, because they think that it removes the choice of the chief executive too far from the people.

On the matter of federalism, supporters of the existing electoral college system favor its blend of national and state power. Proponents of the direct-vote plan argue that, since the President is a national officer, he should be elected by votes counted on a nationwide basis. District-plan supporters, in contrast, believe that the present system has meant moving too far away from state control over elections.

Underlying these favorable and unfavorable attitudes toward a number of very complex issues are varying assumptions about what kind of support a presidential candidate should have in order to be elected. The present electoral college system occupies the middle ground of three fundamental choices: it aggregates the popular vote by entire states rather than by smaller subdivisions or by the country as a whole.

Should the President be chosen simply by a "democratic" majority or by a plurality of the voters, whatever the other consequences? Or should his electoral base be designed to promote other desirable characteristics in the political system as well? Those who support the former principle—and this seems to include all direct-vote plan proponents—must be willing to regard the political implications of the electoral system as irrelevant or at least secondary. To them, the present system is undesirable because it does not insure absolutely that "the people's choice" will always win. For others, assessments of the political effects are decisive. In the next chapter this fundamental issue is considered in a discussion of the direct-vote plan.

☆

Chapter Four

☆

THE DIRECT-VOTE PLAN

THE MOST DRAMATIC PROPOSAL for changing the presidential election system—the direct-vote plan—would eliminate altogether the electoral college, the electoral vote system, and the general-ticket system. It would aggregate the popular votes in the nation as a whole.

While the idea of the direct-vote plan is simple, its implications are complex and uncertain. It would produce major changes in American politics. The President would be elected with a very different mandate than he has today. Accordingly, the direct-vote plan is probably the most controversial method yet devised for electing the President—except perhaps for the electoral college system itself.

The principal direct-vote proposals differ in some details. A draft resolution of the American Bar Association, once endorsed by the late Senate Minority Leader Everett M. Dirksen of Illinois, provides that after congressional approval the direct-vote amendment would be submitted to special ratifying conventions in each state. Some apprehension was expressed at congressional hearings that these conventions might open up a Pandora's box of constitutional amendments. Most advocates of the direct vote favor the usual procedure, ratification by state legislatures, which has been followed in the passage of every constitutional amendment except the repeal of prohibition. The direct-vote plan approved by the House in 1969 would become effective if ratified by three-fourths of the state legislatures within seven years. Under

69

the leading Senate measure,[1] introduced in January 1969 by Senator Birch Bayh and cosponsored by thirty-nine other senators, the direct-vote plan would take effect on the May 1 following ratification by the state legislatures. The amendment passed by the House[2] would make the plan effective one year after the January 21 following ratification—probably a later date than provided in the Bayh amendment and probably not until after the 1972 election. Otherwise, the two measures are substantially identical. The language of the House amendment is cited here.

The House-approved measure provides that each voter shall cast one vote for a ticket of candidates who have agreed to run together for President and Vice President. Voter qualifications would be the same as for elections to the larger house of state legislatures. However, the legislatures could establish more lenient residence qualifications, and Congress could establish uniform residence qualifications for presidential elections. The amendment further provides:

> The pair of persons having the greatest number of votes for President and Vice President shall be elected, if such number be at least 40 per centum of the whole number of votes cast for such offices. If no pair of persons has such number, a runoff election shall be held in which the choice of President and Vice President shall be made from the two pairs of persons who received the highest number of votes.

State legislatures would be empowered to prescribe the time, places, and manner of holding presidential elections and to decide whose names would appear on their own ballots; but Congress could "at any time by law make or alter such regulations" and could make laws about counting returns and making them public. The days on which presidential elections would be held would be set by Congress and would be uniform throughout the country.

1. S.J. Res. 1, in *Electing the President*, Hearings before the Subcommittee on Constitutional Amendments of the Senate Committee on the Judiciary, 91 Cong. 1 sess. (1969), pp. 622–25.
2. H.J. Res. 681, *Congressional Record*, daily ed., Sept. 11, 1969, p. H7823.

Congress would also be authorized to pass legislation dealing with a candidate's death or withdrawal.

Direct-vote proponents argue that this plan is the only one that would assure that the candidate with the most popular votes would win; they contend that the political effects of the change are speculative and, in any event, of secondary importance. We have already explained why we believe that a runner-up President under the existing electoral college system is very unlikely. The extent and desirability of changes in the political system that would result from the direct-vote plan are discussed below. As the plan's advocates emphasize, the direction and magnitude of these changes cannot be predicted accurately. However, we believe there is persuasive evidence that the direct-vote plan would greatly change the patterns of presidential politics; and we oppose many of the developments we foresee, particularly an end to the existing two-party system, a decline in influence for metropolitan areas, and a weakened presidency.

The Political Decline of Metropolitan Areas

Under the direct-vote plan, the most populous states and their metropolitan centers would lose the great strategic importance they have under the electoral college procedure. Of course, populous states would continue to cast more votes than would the smaller states; but abolishing the general-ticket system would eliminate the prize the major states can offer of a large bloc of votes available to the highest bidder.

Accordingly, the direct-vote plan would dramatically shift the relative power of states. The electoral power of each state would no longer depend on the size of its total electoral vote bloc but instead on the size of the popular margin the state gave the winning candidate. The plan would place a premium on areas where a candidate could roll up large popular pluralities. This would mean prominence for a different group of states than the eleven with the most electoral votes under the existing system. Consider which states have given winners the largest popular margins of victory in recent close presidential elections. In 1960 the winning ticket had a plurality of at least 100,000 votes in the following states: Georgia, Indiana, Iowa, Kansas, Louisiana, Massachusetts, Nebraska, New York, Ohio, Oklahoma, Pennsylvania, and Rhode Island. In 1968, states with a 100,000-vote plurality or more were: Alabama, California, Florida, Georgia, Illinois, Indiana, Iowa, Kansas, Louisiana, Massachusetts, Michigan, Minnesota, Mississippi, Nebraska, New York, North Carolina, Oklahoma, Pennsylvania, Rhode Island, Virginia, and the District of Columbia. Thus the direct-vote plan would mean a strategic position for the states that are politically more homogeneous as well as at least fairly populous.

Just as the direct-vote plan would reduce the voting power of the most populous states, it would also end the ability of their metropolitan areas to swing an entire bloc of votes from one column to another. With this change, the metropolis would lose its most important point of leverage in the total political system. Smaller cities, towns, and rural areas would gain relative to metropolitan areas. The sections of greatest strategic value would be those that are the most politically homogeneous and that would produce larger pluralities. The most populous homogeneous areas would be capable of producing the largest pluralities of all.

This loss in power for the major metropolitan areas, and the corresponding rise to prominence of other regions, would have significant effects on public policy. In shaping domestic policy, new forces would be at work. The balance of power in presidential elections would be tipped from the more progressive metropolitan dwellers to the conservatives, who tend to predominate in small towns and rural areas. For similar reasons, the ethnic politics of the presidency would change. Since ethnic groups living in urban and suburban areas would be of less strategic importance, their pressures on policy formulation would be less effective. These groups prominently include Negroes, Jews, Irish, Puerto Ricans, and Italians, among others. For example, how important would the

Negro vote be if it were no longer strategically situated—particularly since it is probably smaller in total than the vote received by George Wallace in 1968? Ethnic groups living in the countryside—southern whites and also southern Negroes, if they voted; and German-, Scandinavian-, and Anglo-Americans in the Midwest and West—would gain new political importance under the direct-vote plan. Again, groups lower in socioeconomic status, who are less likely to vote than are the more affluent, would stand to lose under the direct-vote plan. This is because *voting* would be the basis of representation in the nationwide tally; under the existing system, *population* is the basis of the size of a state's representation in electoral votes.

The effect on foreign policy is less clear. Insofar as the populous states tend more than the rest of the country to be predominantly in favor of American involvement in foreign aid, international organizations, and other forms of civilian activities abroad, the trend would be away from such a policy. The decline in influence of some ethnic groups—most notably the Jews—and the rise of others cited would affect their foreign policy concerns.

A New Political Party System

The direct-vote plan would, in our view, alter the fundamental nature of the American party system. Its impact would be greatest on the number and the internal power structure of the parties.

The direct-vote plan, particularly in combination with the popular runoff provision, would tend to encourage minor party candidacies. So long as there were only two strong parties contesting an election—and particularly so long as the race were not very close—one candidate would win a popular majority and thereby the presidency. However, if there were more than two candidates (and there always are, though under the electoral college system the additional ones have usually had little support), the possibility would be great that in a close contest none would receive a majority. The House direct-vote amendment tries to minimize this possibility by making a 40-percent plurality sufficient to elect a candidate. This proviso may not discourage third parties—especially "spoilers." Any combination of them that received more than 20 percent of the vote could probably force a runoff in a close contest.

What would be the effect of the runoff provision? Since such a system has never been used to choose the President, there is no directly applicable evidence. Scholars must look elsewhere for an answer. The French political scientist Maurice Duverger has written, in his classic book on political parties, that any second-ballot system tends to produce a multiparty situation: "The absence of a second ballot and of further polls, particularly in the presidential election, constitutes in fact one of the historical reasons for the emergence and the maintenance of the two-party system."[3] As a basis for this conclusion, Duverger used an analysis by V. O. Key, Jr. In southern Democratic primaries, Key found, there tended to be more candidates running in elections where there were runoff provisions than in elections where any plurality was enough to win.[4] Thus it appears that a runoff system would encourage minor parties to mount presidential campaigns. The direct-vote plan would not affect the simple-plurality, single-member constituency for seats in legislative bodies, which Duverger and others have viewed as a principal basis of a two-party system. However, even if the two-party congressional pattern continued, this would not mean that several parties might not compete for the presidency. Moreover, as Alexander Heard has written: "The constitutional feature that most determines the nature of the American party system is the method of electing the President."[5] In sum, the runoff provision of the direct-vote amendment would raise the expectations and almost certainly increase the incentives of minor parties

3. Maurice Duverger, *Political Parties* (John Wiley & Sons, 1959), pp. 239–45.
4. V. O. Key, Jr., *Southern Politics in State and Nation* (Alfred A. Knopf, 1949), p. 423.
5. Alexander Heard, *A Two-Party South?* (University of North Carolina Press, 1952), p. 169.

to enter the presidential race and perhaps eventually to enter state and local contests. The Democrats and the Republicans, as the major parties, would lose strength.

Another problem with the runoff device is that it does not necessarily result in victory for the candidate preferred by most voters. In a multiparty contest for the presidency, especially if the leader's margin is slim, candidates who fail to make the runoff may often decide to support the runner-up and so secure final election of the candidate who is the second choice of most voters.[6]

The direct-vote plan would thus pave the way for minor candidates to bargain with contestants in the runoff election. This process does in fact occur in southern Democratic primaries when a runoff is necessary. Those who lose in the first round are wooed by contestants in the runoff election. Under the existing presidential election system, however, the bargaining takes place during the national conventions of the major political parties. Critics of the present system have argued that it permits such bargaining in the electoral college or in the House; but because of the two-party norm it has helped establish, the bargaining actually takes place earlier, at the conventions. Under the direct-vote plan, in contrast, the minor candidates might often have and would doubtless use the opportunity to bargain during the interim between the first election and the runoff contest.

We consider convention bargaining preferable in the kind of politics it entails. The coalition supporting the nominees is now developed in the reasonably open processes of preconvention and convention politics and is well publicized during the days when the delegates are gathered together. The nature of this coalition is clear to the attentive citizenry at least from the time of the convention; barring extraordinary circumstances, it is essentially the same coalition throughout the campaign. With a runoff system, bargaining would be different. It would not take place at a nationally

6. On the theoretical aspects of this problem, see Paul T. David, "Reforming the Presidential Nominating Process," *Law and Contemporary Problems*, Vol. 27 (Spring 1962), pp. 161–64.

televised event, at which the political leaders involved would be
questioned by reporters and viewed by the public. The many small
bargains made would not, by the very nature of the process, be
subject to public scrutiny. The "smoke-filled rooms" that stigma-
tized conventions of bygone eras would once again be the locale
for the crucial phase of presidential selection. Opportunity would
be diminished for the average voter to inform himself about presidential politics. Indeed, the importance of bargaining after the first
contest might become so great that the initial race would in effect
become the real nominating process. The national party convention, the major bulwark of the two principal parties today, might
become little more than a tactical skirmish in a lengthened campaign.

The direct-vote plan, of course, need not contain a runoff provision. Some proponents of this plan would prefer that the President
be elected by a simple popular plurality. Under this procedure,
"spoilers" would no longer be able to delay an election decision.
However, they could reduce the winner's national plurality as far
as possible, and they might be able to draw votes from one candidate in order to elect his principal opponent. Under the existing
system they can do this only on a state-by-state basis; historically,
their impact in these terms has been rare. Election by a plurality
in a multiparty contest, as in a popular runoff election, could mean
the election of a candidate other than the one preferred by most
voters. The plurality winner might simply be the candidate whose
supporters' loyalties were most constant.

Other contingency election procedures have been included in
some recent direct-vote plans. An amendment offered by Democratic Senator Joseph D. Tydings of Maryland and Republican
Senator Robert P. Griffin of Michigan[7] provides that if no one won
a 40-percent popular plurality, a majority of the electoral votes,
awarded on the same basis as at present, would be sufficient to
elect; if there were still no winner, Congress in joint session voting

7. See *Congressional Record*, daily ed., June 18, 1970, pp. S9299 and S9335.

as individuals would choose the President. Under the "federal system" plan offered by Democratic Senator Thomas F. Eagleton of Missouri and Republican Senator Robert Dole of Kansas,[8] any popular plurality would be sufficient to elect, provided the leading candidate carried (1) states comprising at least half the total number of voters, or (2) more than half the states, or (3) a majority of electoral votes, awarded as at present. Otherwise, electoral votes of minor candidates would be divided among the top two contestants in proportion to their showing in each state, thereby producing an electoral vote majority winner and President.

Both the Tydings-Griffin and the Eagleton-Dole plans are aimed at preventing interference by minor parties with the rendering of a clear-cut presidential verdict. To this end, both couple the direct-vote principle with ultimate resort to a scheme much like that under the existing system. This suggests that the present electoral vote general-ticket system may be vital to the achievement of a broadly based presidential constituency. Moreover, both plans, particularly the Eagleton-Dole proposal, are undesirably complex. Their various possible grounds for presidential victory are also somewhat contradictory in theory, and conceivably in practice. Both plans are considerably more cumbersome and difficult to understand than either the Bayh amendment or the existing system.

Adoption of the direct-vote plan would thus affect the status of minor parties, helping some and hurting others. Abandonment of the state general-ticket system would reduce the leverage of minor parties with swing vote strength—the New York Liberals, for example, or other locally significant parties. The same would be true in a lesser degree of parties capable of capturing some electoral votes on a state or regional basis—for example, Strom Thurmond's 1948 Dixiecrats. Instead, another kind of minor party would stand to benefit: the party with significant, though minority, strength across the country. George Wallace's party may be the forerunner of such a group. A party on the left could become

8. See *ibid.*, July 14, 1970, p. S11249

equally relevant. A presidential candidacy might make sense strategically for any number of political groups with a shared supraregional interest. Chances for impact would be increased if minor parties mounted campaigns for, and won, a substantial number of congressional, state, and local offices. The problem would be particularly serious if "spoiler" minor parties, intent on sabotaging the system altogether, worked to maximize their new opportunity. While the two-party tradition seems strong today, we believe that if the rules were changed to benefit minor parties, as under the direct-vote plan, the two-party system might be seriously and even permanently eroded.

Under the direct-vote plan, political parties would also become more homogeneous. More extreme groups, and perhaps groups particularly concerned with one issue or set of issues, would leave the major parties to more moderate forces. Minor party strength and remaining major party support would presumably be drawn from particular social, regional, and ideological strata. The Democrats and Republicans today, of course, are each relatively stronger among certain population groups; but the lines of both geography and ideology are blurred. Presidential contests under the direct-vote plan would mean a new set of coalitions, perhaps resulting in a fairly clear-cut spectrum from left to right: New Left, Democrats, Republicans, Wallace party—each with distinct social strongholds and philosophical boundaries.

The direct-vote plan would also affect the internal structure of the major parties. With the demise of the general-ticket system, state leaders would become less important in presidential politics. Similarly, ending the swing vote power of major metropolitan areas would reduce the influence of their local leaders. Consider the difference in their importance under the existing system and under the direct-vote plan. At present, Illinois has 26 electoral votes, nearly 5 percent of the total of 538. A powerful leader in Illinois, or even in Cook County (Chicago), can produce enough popular votes to carry the state and with it 5 percent of the total electoral votes. In 1964, for example, Cook County cast 2,432,899 votes for President, more than half the Illinois total of 4,702,841. Similar situations exist in other populous states. As a result, governors, mayors, and other leaders who can deliver the vote have enjoyed influence within their national parties, particularly in presidential elections. Under the direct-vote plan, the efforts of the same major state leader would produce only a very small proportion of the 70 million or more total popular votes cast. The Cook County total of 2,432,899 in 1964, for example, was only 3.0 percent of the total national vote for President that year of 70,644,592. State and especially local leaders would not be rendered completely powerless under the direct-vote plan; they would still be able to mobilize sizable blocs of popular votes. But the blocs of votes they could potentially swing would represent a smaller proportion of the total vote. The levers of power would essentially be operated by national leaders. As state lines became irrelevant in aggregating the votes, the national leaders could go to Nebraska or Oregon or Tennessee, as well as to Illinois and similar states, to get their votes. Effective year-round national party or at least candidate organizations would arise. Below the national level, the most important political leaders in presidential politics would be those with a firm grip on the areas more homogeneous in a partisan sense—the "bosses" not just in big cities but throughout the country.

The decline in the strategic importance of metropolitan areas would affect both nominations and campaigns. There would be less incentive to nominate candidates from large states, though we have noted that this tradition may already be declining. In campaigning, more reliance on television would increase an existing trend toward more national appeals. Under the direct-vote plan, there would be relatively less direct attention to populous states and metropolitan centers and relatively more effort elsewhere. Politically homogeneous areas, which are often sparsely populated sections, would receive increased attention.

Party competition would be at zenith with adoption of the direct-vote plan. Clearly the day of the safe state would be done; it is

probably done in any event. All parties would be encouraged to
campaign anywhere they thought they could win votes, and each
vote would be counted in one national tally.

For various reasons, including the possibility of a runoff, campaigns would become more expensive. We have already suggested
that television would be used more; the purchase of costly network
time is the largest item in any campaign budget. Particularly in
close contests, spending might soar tremendously. This new strain
on party treasuries might mean added pressures for subsidy of presidential candidates by the federal government. Increasing costs
would intensify political turmoil, possibly affecting the presidency
as an institution and public attitudes toward it.

The political effects of the direct-vote plan would almost certainly shift the balance among the parties, perhaps particularly
within the major parties. The overall impact is hard to predict because many forces would be at work. Our assumptions are that the
growth of minor party strength would weaken the major parties
about equally, that candidate and issue orientations could help or
hurt either major party, and that either could successfully woo new
voters. The decline of the metropolitan bloc would be the most
important change. For several decades liberal, urban Democrats
and progressive, urban-suburban Republicans have tended to domi-
nate presidential politics; they would lose influence under the
direct-vote plan.

The most significant impact in partisan terms would come from
the decline in power of the most populous states and the principal
metropolitan centers. Central city and suburban areas would not
be completely eclipsed because they contain many votes con-
veniently concentrated for campaign purposes. But they would lose
the state general-ticket system, the most powerful weapon in their
political arsenal. The direct-vote plan would eliminate that system
without eliminating, for example, equal representation of the states
in the Senate or the minimum of one House seat for each state,
both of which tend to overrepresent nonmetropolitan areas. As the
major population centers lost influence, so would the factions that

are strongest within them—liberal Democrats and progressive Republicans.

Accordingly, forces representing more politically homogeneous areas, often small town and rural sections and often conservative, would become more important within the Republican party. In an era when attention to metropolitan problems is a major point of liberal-conservative cleavage, the political decline of metropolitan areas in presidential elections would mean a parallel decline for progressive Republicans. Safer states of the Midwest, West, and perhaps the South would assume new strategic significance for Republican leaders.

Central-city and populous-state forces now prominent in the Democratic party would face a similar problem. The cities they represent would continue to have important political advantages. They would still produce more votes, particularly more Democratic votes, than would the less densely populated areas; it would still be easier to mobilize urban voters than to get voters to the polls in sparsely settled areas. But clearly the major cities and their leaders would no longer be so preeminent in the Democratic party as they are today. Metropolitan leaders outside the presently most important states would gain new influence. In addition, with the abolition of the general-ticket system, the homogeneity of rural and small town areas would be a political virtue under the direct-vote plan. The Democrats might direct more attention to such areas.

What would this new party system mean for the voters? Their overall motivations would be unlikely to change. They would continue to cast their votes on the bases of party, candidates, and issues. However, when state lines were no longer a factor in presidential elections, there might be a tendency for social class and policy views to become more important in voting decisions because social and ideological factions with nationwide strength would be more likely to organize parties.

While the direct-vote plan would mean that each ballot would count equally in tallying the returns, it would not mean that each voter would be equally affected directly by the presidential campaign. Whatever the system for aggregating votes, the use of network television would still tend to orient campaigns toward a national audience. In personal campaigning, though, the plan would mean less concentration on the dozen or so largest states and their principal metropolitan areas. The more populous of the politically homogeneous areas would gain particularly, and the heterogeneous major metropolitan areas in the states that are now most powerful would lose greatly. The candidates would still be unlikely to visit Velva, North Dakota; but a visit to Fargo might be more likely.

The direct-vote plan would tend to make the electorate more politically minded. Every vote would now theoretically "count." There would be extensive canvassing in party strongholds particularly. Parties other than the one that is predominant locally would also have reason to go into action. Campaign managers from all parties—most certainly the Democrats, who apparently have the allegiance of more nonvoters than do the Republicans—would work to increase the turnout. The potential benefit in civic education is considerable. It is doubtful, however, that there would actually be a marked impact on most nonvoters, who are usually those least interested in politics.

A Fragile Presidency

A major objective of the direct-vote plan is to assure legitimacy to the presidency by making certain that the candidate with the most popular votes wins. Historically, the plan would apparently have changed the outcomes of several elections, although there is no assurance that this difference would have strengthened the presidency or its incumbent. On balance, we think the direct-vote plan would weaken the presidency for a number of reasons.

The direct-vote plan would do away with possible disruptions over runner-up Presidents, faithless electors, and unscrupulous bargaining in the electoral college or in the House. It would eliminate all the technical difficulties of translating electoral votes into popular votes—the state general-ticket system, possible discrepancies between voter turnout and population (on the basis of which electoral votes, in addition to the minimum of three, are awarded), and discrepancies between the size of the population as of election day and that recorded in the last census (used for electoral vote purposes).

Would such changes have meant the election of different Presidents in the past? If the popular votes actually cast were counted under the rules of the direct-vote plan, and if it is assumed that other factors would have been constant, different Presidents would have been selected at least twice since 1824, when popular vote totals began to be reliably recorded. In 1876 Samuel J. Tilden, with a popular vote percentage of 50.9, would evidently have defeated Rutherford B. Hayes (47.9 percent). In 1888 Grover Cleveland, with 48.6 percent of the popular vote, would probably have beaten Benjamin Harrison, who had 47.8 percent. The situation might also have been different in 1860, when Abraham Lincoln—not on the ballot in ten states—won an electoral college majority while leading in popular votes with only 39.8 percent of the total. If the popular vote result had been the same under the direct-vote plan, there would have been a runoff election between Lincoln and Stephen A. Douglas, who came in second with 29.4 percent of the popular total.

These historical projections, however, must be viewed with some skepticism. The effective difference between the existing system and the direct-vote plan has not been very significant. Only in the 1888 election did a popular vote winner lose because of the electoral college system. It is shown in Chapter 3 that because of the decline of one-party states, a runner-up President under the existing system is far less likely today than in the 1880s.

Moreover, the probable proliferation of minor party candidacies under the direct-vote plan makes speculation about past contests problematical. In a race with three or four or more significant candidates, none of whom wins a 40-percent plurality, a candidate could finish second in the first election and win the runoff. This phenomenon occurs with some frequency in southern primaries. Such a pattern, particularly as it continued over time, would undercut the presidential mandate and perhaps even threaten the stability of the system itself.

The direct-vote plan would also tend to weaken the presidency because it might often mean a prolonged period of indecision about the outcome of an election. If, as we anticipate, the encouragement of minor party candidacies should mean frequent runoff contests, the period of time needed to carry on the presidential election would be lengthened. In addition, the process of counting the votes might also be prolonged. In close races, the total number of ballots would have to be established before it could be calculated whether any ticket had won 40 percent of the total. The outcome might depend on absentee ballots. Surely political leaders would be tempted to demand recounts. Delays could be far more serious than any anxieties that exist now about the procedures under the present system.

There is also some evidence that a proliferation of candidacies might mean more irresponsible appeals to the electorate—another unhealthy development for both the presidency and the political system. Maurice Duverger notes that rabble-rousing is more common in parties without "a majority bent" and the potential responsibility of governing.[9] Under the direct-vote plan, as under the present system, opportunity for a demagogue would lie primarily in his ability to play the spoiler, keeping either major candidate from winning the requisite support and peddling his influence thereafter. It is remotely conceivable that under the direct-vote plan an irresponsible candidate with an appealing personality and an appealing issue could possibly capture particular disaffected social strata and win a 40-percent plurality of the popular vote; or, more probably, such a candidate could force a runoff in which the runner-up would win. It is virtually impossible for him to have that much influence under the present system.

9. Duverger, *op. cit.*, p. 285.

The direct-vote plan might also mean less acceptance of the electoral verdict by the citizens. With more parties and more emphasis on turnout, the level of intensity of political conviction might be greater; as a result, more people would be more unwilling to lose. An additional and perhaps more ominous possibility is that disaffected residents of major cities, especially Negroes, might feel resentful because their relative power had been decreased. People roused from their lethargy, disbelief, and apprehension by exhortations to vote might be profoundly disillusioned if they lost in a close and hard-fought race, especially if they lost in a runoff in which the first-round leader finished second.

The direct-vote plan would also tend to narrow the constituency base of the presidency. In addition to making contingency elections more frequent, the direct-vote plan would make election by 40 percent of the voters legal. Under the existing system, presidential candidates must appeal to a wide number of interests and groups and must develop support throughout the country. The direct-vote plan would make one-issue, or one-stratum, Presidents possible. A Democrat might win, for example, by promising urban dwellers that he would save their decaying cities. Or a Republican might win by appealing to suburbanites chafing under taxes or inflation or worried about law and order. Or a candidate exploiting the peace issue might be able to muster 40 percent of the votes. The actual support for such a President might prove to be shallow; his coalition might extend no further than the issue on which he was elected.

For these reasons, the direct-vote plan would weaken the presidency. Encouraging minor parties, making election outcomes closer, and eliminating the President's solid mandate to govern would all adversely affect the position of the President taking office and perhaps his subsequent tenure as well. Winning with only a plurality of the vote, and certainly winning only after a runoff contest, would mean that the President assumed power with a precarious constituency base. This inauspicious beginning would hardly help him in dealings with Congress, the bureaucracy, and foreign governments. Indeed, after a relatively poor showing at the polls, such a President might well be forced to go to influential members of those institutions in search of support. Anyone elected by a narrow margin takes office with a poor bargaining position; but we believe that the direct-vote plan could put a President in the White House with a far narrower base of support than is possible under the existing system.

Proponents of the direct vote take issue with this point. They note that most state governors are elected under the popular plurality system, that few of them are contested by more than one serious opponent, that most win a popular majority, and that there is little evidence of weakness in those elected by only a plurality. Yet a governorship and the presidency have differing attractions for aspiring political leaders. The United States has more political variety and talent than does any individual state. We think, therefore, that the national chief executive office, as compared with the state chief executive office, should attract more candidates with leadership capability and substantial popular backing. Moreover, so few governors have been elected with less than a 40-percent plurality (none since the Second World War) that there are not enough cases on which to rest a firm conclusion about their effectiveness in office. In the larger number of cases where public officials have won narrow victories, their peers and associates have tended to regard them at least initially with considerable skepticism. Lyndon Johnson, for example, was nicknamed "Landslide Lyndon" by the Senate majority leader after Johnson won a Senate seat largely because of an 87-vote victory in the 1948 runoff primary in Texas. Others have made equally bad initial impressions on their colleagues because of scant voter support. Johnson's case shows that a man can overcome such a handicap; but the handicap itself is hardly beneficial to the man.

National Administration of Presidential Elections

The direct-vote plan would also affect relationships within the federal system. Essentially it would serve to strengthen the power of the national government and weaken that of the states in presidential election procedures.

The whole thrust of the direct-vote plan would be national because the outcome would depend entirely on the popular vote in the country as a whole. State borders would be irrelevant in aggregating the votes. The President and Vice President would be chosen by all the nation's voters, with each vote counting equally, regardless of location.

The direct-vote plan would eliminate the authority a state government now has to decide what kind of presidential electoral system it will use. As was noted above, this authority is no longer very significant, since the general-ticket system is all but universal.

What is far more important is that the national government would intervene directly in the administration of presidential elections, which is now a state function. Under the existing system, the federal government established the basic rules for presidential elections in 1804 in the Twelfth Amendment to the Constitution and has in recent years attempted to guarantee the right of a maximum number of American citizens to vote in federal elections. State governments carry on the actual duties of administering elections. Under the direct-vote plan, this pattern would have to change over time. Candidates for President and Vice President would still have to get on the ballot in individual states unless, as we anticipate, federal standards of eligibility were established. The direct-vote amendment passed by the House specifically gives Congress a new reserve power in this field. State governments, at least initially, would be in charge of supervising elections within their boundaries, certifying the returns, and forwarding them to Washington for the official count. But the direct-vote amendment approved by the House contains a provision permitting Congress to move into election administration. It is difficult to envision how the system could work without some federal supervision to ensure an honest count. If the national total determined the winner, a national authority logically should administer the tallying of returns, just as individual state authorities administer the statewide returns under the existing system. But might not an incumbent administration be tempted to count the votes in its own favor? This dilemma has been given little public notice by proponents of the plan. They presumably would argue that national election officials would be no more venal than their state counterparts, and perhaps less so. Yet even under a civil service system federal officials would be the employees of the national administration in power, whereas state employees work for governments that may be allied either for or against the national incumbents. In addition, federal residence requirements, which may be established by Congress under the amendment passed by the House, also seem to us to be a logical outgrowth of the direct-vote proposal and one aspect of its provisions that we would favor.

A Middle Ground?

The direct-vote plan and the existing electoral college system have been the alternatives in the recent electoral reform debate. Curiously, and perhaps stubbornly, proponents and opponents of the direct-vote plan have talked past each other, each group concerning itself primarily with the merits of its own system and particularly with the failings of the other major option.

Thus, active supporters of the direct-vote measure, many of whom were prominent participants in the reapportionment and voting rights struggles of the 1950s and 1960s, have tended to emphasize the one-person-one-vote principle in making their case. They have stressed that it is not a partisan cause, but one of equity and good government. They have argued that any effects that the change would have on the political system are impossible to predict, of lesser importance, and indeed perhaps unworthy considerations for those seeking to design an ideal method of choosing the leader of the United States government.

Various critics of the direct-vote plan have objected to it on various grounds. One set of criticisms is political. Liberal opponents of the change have worried that the metropolitan areas, where most liberal leaders and their constituencies live, would lose their favorable position of access to the presidency. Conservative opponents of the plan have suspected that the measure is simply another way of extending the already long arm of the federal government further into state affairs—in this instance, into the administration of elections.

These political criticisms of the direct-vote plan are based on an assumption also made by those academic students of government, including the authors of this book, who find fault with the plan. This is the assumption, elaborated earlier, that such a fundamental change, regardless of whether the motivations of its sponsors were public-spirited or self-interested, would significantly change the political system, perhaps for the worse. Analysis of these effects has generated academic criticism of the direct-vote plan because of its potential impact on the party system, the presidency, and the balance of power between metropolitan and nonmetropolitan areas.

During the course of the debate the two streams of criticism have merged; academicians have political views, and politicians have made use of academic arguments. What have not merged are the sets of issues about which the two sides in the electoral reform debate are arguing. Proponents of the direct vote claim that their plan is the only alternative that would assure the desired objectives; opponents argue that it is inescapably flawed with undesirable side effects. Is there no way of satisfying the concerns of both camps? Could a way be found to avoid both the dangers of the existing electoral college system, which are known but remote, and the hazards of the direct-vote plan, less certain yet more threatening? To begin to answer those questions, the other electoral reform plans that have been put forward in recent years to perfect the method of selecting the President must be considered.

☆

Chapter Five

☆

THE AUTOMATIC PLAN

THE MOST MODEST MEASURE suggested by proponents of electoral college reform is the automatic plan. It aims at maintaining the present system approximately as it now operates while correcting two supposed defects—the electoral college itself and the contingency election procedure. The plan is thus widely acceptable; it has been opposed mainly by those who believe it does not go far enough. It has been supported by at least two recent Presidents, many members of Congress, and various observers of the American political scene. The automatic plan would continue for the foreseeable future most political effects of the existing system, although the various contingency election schemes attached to individual automatic plans might provide slight variations. The automatic plan is quite similar to the system it seeks to perfect in its underlying assumptions about the desirable kind of electoral base for a President.

Fundamentally, the automatic plan would work exactly like the present procedure except that the office of presidential elector would be abolished and all of each state's electoral votes would be automatically awarded to the ticket that carried its popular vote for President. In the language of an amendment introduced in the House in 1969 by Democratic Representative Hale Boggs of Louisiana, the House majority whip,[1]

1. H.J. Res. 1, in *Electoral College Reform*, Hearings before the House Committee on the Judiciary, 91 Cong. 1 sess. (1969), pp. 665–68.

The President and Vice President shall be elected by the people of each State in such manner as the legislature thereof may direct, and by the people of the District [of Columbia] . . . in such manner as the Congress shall by law prescribe. The Congress may determine the time of the election of the President and Vice President, which day shall be the same throughout the United States. In such an election, a vote may be cast only as a joint vote for the election of two persons (referred to in this article as a "presidential candidacy") one of whom has consented that his name appear as candidate for President on the ballot with the name of the other as candidate for Vice President, and the other of whom has consented that his name appear as candidate for Vice President on the ballot with the name of the said candidate for President. No person may consent to have his name appear on the ballot with more than one other person. No person constitutionally ineligible to the office of President shall be eligible to that of Vice President. . . .

Each State shall be entitled to a number of electoral votes for each of the offices of President and Vice President equal to the whole number of Senators and Representatives to which such State may be entitled in the Congress. The District [of Columbia] shall be entitled to a number of electoral votes . . . equal to the whole number of Senators and Representatives in Congress to which the District would be entitled if it were a State, but in no event more than the least populous State. In the case of each State and the District, the presidential candidacy receiving the greatest number of [popular] votes shall be entitled to the whole number of electoral votes of such State or District.

This amendment would initiate several specific changes. First, each state's popular vote result would control its electoral votes, as it does in practice but not necessarily in theory today. Second, Congress would be more broadly empowered to regulate presidential elections, as it is already empowered under Article II of the Constitution to set the time and day for the choice of electors. In addition, the winner-take-all, state general-ticket system would be written into the Constitution. Presidential and vice presidential candidates would be required to run as a publicly announced ticket. And the automatic plan could, as the Boggs measure does, contain provisions requiring the presidential and vice presidential candidates to run and be elected as a ticket and, more important, empowering Congress to deal with the death or withdrawal of a candidate and a possible tie in electoral votes.[2]

Several alternative ways of making the contingency election procedure more "democratic" have also been included in recently proposed automatic plans. In the Boggs measure a 40-percent electoral vote plurality would be sufficient to elect a presidential ticket. If no candidate won such a plurality, there would be a runoff popular election between the two tickets receiving the most electoral votes. Again, Democratic Representative Jonathan B. Bingham of New York in 1968 introduced an automatic plan calling for a popular runoff election between the top two candidates if there were no electoral vote majority; the latter proposal would thus require a greater margin of victory than the 40-percent plurality of the Boggs plan. Republican Representative Thomas S. Kleppe of North Dakota in 1969 introduced an automatic plan under which the popular vote winners would be designated President and Vice President if no ticket received a majority of the electoral votes. Some political leaders have advocated keeping the contingency elections in Congress but requiring a majority vote of a joint session, with each member having one vote. Others have proposed that the House alone make the choice, on a one-member-one-vote basis. Still others have urged that if the choice does go to Congress, the presidential contest be narrowed from the three candidates with the most electoral votes to the two highest.

Essentially, the automatic plan would mean only marginal change in the political system as well as in the electoral system. To a certain degree, it would foster increased party loyalty. The automatic plan itself would involve little change in the balance of political power. Some contingency election proposals, however, would have additional impact, in various directions.

2. Obviously, under this provision a certain amount of political power would accrue to Congress and also to any group given authority to choose the President or Vice President or to move into the vacuum. However, there is little likelihood that the authority would be invoked.

More Party Loyalty?

In abolishing the office of presidential elector, the automatic plan would eliminate a device by which state and local party leaders may withhold support from national party candidates to whom they are opposed. However, such maneuvers have had very little impact on past elections. Since 1789, only six electors have been "faithless," and only fourteen unpledged electors have been chosen.

What would be the response of dissident state and local leaders? Under the plan, their only choices would be to support their party's national candidate, however repugnant to them he was; to support the other major party's candidate; to back a third candidate, perhaps using the regular party emblem on the ballot; or to boycott the election altogether.

Would the automatic plan encourage state party dissidents to support third-party movements? The 1948 Dixiecrats, the 1960 unpledged elector movement, and the 1968 Wallace party provide ample precedent but scant encouragement for would-be organizers of minor parties. Conceivably, the American Independent party might spell the beginning of the end for the two-party system; but in the absence of further changes in the political system, it seems unlikely. Wallace's showing in 1968 provides a narrow base for the future. In addition, a minor party would have to elect senators, congressmen, and lesser officials in the coming years, and build a lasting party organization as well. What seems more likely to us is a gradual party realignment in the South. Among older politicians there will be few conversions; but an increasing number of young southern conservatives will probably become Republicans, and a growing proportion of young southern Democrats will probably be liberals. Wallace supporters will tend to divide between the two groups along economic and social class lines.

Given this analysis, it is apparent that under the automatic plan, the situation for minor parties would remain much the same as it is at present. Their main opportunity to affect presidential politics would be within particular states or regions. A minor party might serve as a local substitute for the possibility of unpledged electors, which would be eliminated. And it would still be remotely possible for a minor party to carry a few states or to swing a state and even an election to one of the major party candidates. But that would be the extent of minor-party influence on the electoral outcome.

In headier moments, some enthusiastic proponents of the automatic plan have hoped that abolishing possibly disloyal electors would ensure, or at least encourage, loyalty from dissident state party leaders. To put it another way, they hoped that the automatic plan would bring about greater homogeneity within the major parties, at least in national election years. The plan would work to the disadvantage of right-wing Republicans and unreconstructed southern Democrats, who have tried (largely unsuccessfully) to manipulate electors in recent years. However, as noted above, state party leaders would be left with a variety of options other than to support the national ticket. Only as the most extreme of these leaders formally cut ties with the national party would the party become more homogeneous; and the present ties of this faction are nominal. While abolishing the means of sabotaging the national party in the electoral college would end this potential leverage of state and local leaders, it would hardly assure their working loyalty or end their influence on the fortunes of national candidates within their states. State and local leaders would continue to be powerful party members, carefully cultivated by those taking part in the presidential campaign.

The Political System as Usual

Substituting an automatic casting of electoral votes for balloting by human electors would have little further effect on the political system. The automatic plan would maintain the metropolitan emphasis of the electoral college system, its balance of national and state powers, its fostering of an independent President with a strong constituency base, and its support of the existing political party system.

A switch to the automatic plan would not change the current relative strength of large and small states, and metropolitan and nonmetropolitan areas. The most populous states would remain dominant in electoral votes, although small states would continue to be assured representation by a minimum of three votes. The major metropolitan areas of the most favored states would continue to enjoy decisive influence. The policies of presidential candidates, which are oriented primarily toward the interests of those living in the metropolitan areas of the populous states, would still tend to be liberal and internationalist and solicitous of minority-group concerns.

Nor would there be any weakening of the presidency under the automatic plan. If anything, the institution would be strengthened. The factors involved in electing the President would remain the same. The Chief Executive would continue to be the choice of the popular votes, aggregated by states. The electoral vote outcome would still not be a perfect reflection of the popular vote outcome; it would still be remotely possible for the popular winner to lose. But as was shown in Chapter 3, the existing general-ticket electoral vote system makes the election of the leader in popular votes a virtual certainty even in the closest of contests, as in 1960 and 1968; and the automatic plans being considered would make that system mandatory.

Continuation of the existing electoral vote system would also mean that a long period of doubt about the outcome of an election would remain very improbable. Under the present system, resort to any contingency election procedure has been extremely rare and has not been necessary for well over a century. Moreover, the automatic plan would remove one source of possible unrest: faithless and unpledged electors. Though their impact has not been great in past elections, foreclosing the option of manipulating electors would reassure many who are closely concerned with presidential elections.

The automatic plan might even strengthen the position of the President in carrying out the duties of his office. National party

nominees would be assured of the electoral votes of the states
whose popular votes they had won. Presidents—who almost always are, have been, or will be nominees of major parties—would
no longer have to worry about faithless or unpledged electors.

Adoption of the automatic plan would also mean little change in
the existing balance of state and national powers. States would be
assured of a continuing role in choosing the President. But electoral votes would have to be aggregated by states; individual states
would no longer have the largely theoretical power to determine
the procedure for casting their electoral votes. As we have seen,
national parties would be modestly strengthened, but state leaders
would retain a key strategic role. In other respects, the automatic
plan would maintain the present national-state division of power.
For example, state control of election administration would continue, and federal voting rights laws would remain on the books.

Other than the party loyalty factor already discussed, the automatic plan would have no particular ramifications for the political
party system. If the electoral vote system with the general-ticket
system were maintained, there would be little independent reason
for changing the pattern of nominating primarily candidates from
the more populous states. Nor would the likely effects of the automatic plan on campaign strategy and tactics be great. The electoral
vote system would not be changed except in Maine, which would
have to abandon its new district plan. This would mean a possible
change of only one or two electoral votes, since the state's electors
total only four and either of the winners of the two at-large seats
would almost certainly have carried at least one of the two districts. The relative strength of various states would remain the
same. In the region most affected, the South, rebel Democrats
might simply turn from their party to a minor party in a temporary
aberration from the two-party tradition. In any case, the strategies
of regular Democrats and Republicans would probably be no different from recent patterns. The only perceptible direct effect of
the automatic plan on the balance of power between the major
parties would occur if it led to a serious and lasting minor party

movement or movements, which we find extremely unlikely. Finally, the automatic plan would mean little change in the effects of presidential elections on the citizenry. People would still vote for some combination of party, candidates, and issues; voters in the same populous states and major metropolitan areas would still tend to receive more direct attention from the national candidates.

Contingency Election Plans

The myriad of contingency election procedures added to various automatic plans holds divergent implications for the political system. But any such effects would generally be slight, if not wholly theoretical, because under the general-ticket electoral vote system, which the automatic plan would continue, there have been no contingency elections at all since 1837. Yet because important attention has been given them in the policy debate and because the direction of their effects, however infrequent, could be significant, the contingency election plans merit individual consideration here.

A popular runoff contest in the event no candidate received enough electoral votes to win would mean the greatest deviation from the existing system. The Boggs amendment, which would permit election of a President by a 40-percent electoral vote plurality, is not likely to bring about a contingency election situation. The Bingham amendment, which requires an absolute majority of the electoral vote, would be more likely to generate a runoff.

Whatever the measure of victory needed in the initial contest, a popular runoff system would, when used, have pronounced political effects, which are discussed in more detail in Chapter 4. Above all, it would tend to encourage additional candidates, particularly "spoilers," to enter the race. They would hope to prevent a victory in the initial contest and to be a bargaining force, or even a participant in the runoff—a kind of influence that is very unlikely under the present system, where Democrats and Republicans in Congress would choose the President if the initial vote were inconclusive. This propensity toward minor party influence would probably be minimized under automatic plans, such as that in the Boggs amendment, that decrease the likelihood of bringing about a runoff situation. Similarly, automatic plans containing a runoff provision would probably provide less incentive to spoilers than would a direct-vote plan with a runoff; the general-ticket electoral vote system tends to give a wider margin of victory, more certainly 40 or 50 percent of the total, than does a simple popular vote. The problem of spoilers, who might make a runoff necessary, would also mean weakening the presidency, despite the fact that the presumed motivation for the runoff provision is to enhance the legitimacy of the winner by assuring him a popular majority in the second contest. The runoff contest would indeed serve to liberate the President from the possible stigma of owing his election to members of Congress. It would also eliminate the advantage that less populous states and nonmetropolitan areas have under the existing contingency election process, whereby the House votes by state delegations on a one-state-one-vote basis. Much more important, however, is the fact that the impact of the spoilers (especially under the requirement of an electoral vote majority) would tend to decrease the overall mandate of the President by narrowing his personal constituency in the initial contest and to lengthen the period of uncertainty about the election outcome by bringing about the need for a runoff.

Continuing to vest the powers of contingency election in Congress but reforming its voting procedures would have more limited and, we think, more salutary effects. Providing for a joint session of Congress, with members voting as individuals, or for the House alone voting as individuals, would have approximately the same implications. Both would give a net advantage to the most populous states and metropolitan areas because population, as well as state sovereignty, would affect the allocation of congressional votes. Including representation for the District of Columbia in such a contingency election scheme would redound to the benefit of big-city interests and minority groups, particularly Negroes. It would also set a precedent useful to those who favor home rule and representation in Congress for the District.

Narrowing the choice of Congress to the top two candidates would probably tend to discourage spoilers and other minor candidates. The House or a joint session, voting as individuals, would also facilitate rapid agreement on the winner, thus providing a smoother transition and supporting the institution of the presidency. The President chosen would owe his office at least partially to members of Congress; but he would be able to act independently thereafter. Moreover, if the choice were limited to the two candidates with most popular support, the vote would almost surely be along straight party lines, permitting very little discretion on the part of individual members of Congress.

Designating as the winner the presidential ticket that received the most popular votes, instead of holding any contingency election if there were no electoral vote majority, would end the inequities of the existing rules and eliminate opportunities for bargaining in the House. It would probably discourage minor party candidacies. It would produce a rapid and clear-cut decision about the election outcome by obviating any need for a second contest. It would almost certainly produce a President with a solid popular mandate to govern. While it is remotely possible that the leader in the electoral vote might lose because he had fewer popular votes, this would be most unlikely because of the apparent tendency of the general-ticket system to enlarge the popular plurality winner's margin in electoral votes.

Designating the winner of a plurality of the electoral vote as President would have similar but in our opinion less beneficial results. Like a provision to designate as President the winner of the popular vote, it would eliminate all the problems concerned with the House voting procedure. Its potential impact on minor parties is uncertain; presumably the major parties would have a monopoly on winning, but perhaps not always, since the number of electoral votes required for victory would be less. Again, the plan would probably mean a quick decision in most years. But what if there were a tie? Like the present system, designation of the electoral vote winner could also mean that the presidency would depend on the outcome in a single state. The ultimate winner in a close, particularly a multiparty, contest might have very narrow popular support; with more minor party activity, chances would be greater that he would not be the popular plurality winner.

Is Marginal Change Desirable?

Essentially, the automatic plan has the merits of the existing general-ticket electoral vote system without its defects. In political terms, it would maintain the metropolitan constituency of the President, buttress the two-party system and the federal system, and assure the Chief Executive the solid base of popular support required to govern. The desirability of these patterns is fully discussed in Chapter 3. The automatic plan would simply provide these benefits without the costs inherent in human electors and the present contingency election procedure. For the latter, various possible substitutes have been included in particular automatic plans. Their importance is primarily technical, because they are unlikely to be needed.

The major question that remains about the automatic plan is whether the small amount of change it entails justifies the effort required to pass a constitutional amendment. Proponents consider the narrow scope of the plan a virtue. It is better to change the Constitution as little as possible, proponents say; that way, unexpected side effects are less likely. They add that the principal shortcomings of the existing system can be corrected by a few small changes: elimination of electors who might possibly be disloyal to the voters; perhaps a change in the contingency election procedure; and new provisions to cover the case of a candidate's death. Just a few details should be attended to, they argue, in order to tidy up a basically sound system that might be changed for the worse unless perfected.

Opponents of the plan do not think so. Most favor more far-reaching reform. They seriously doubt that the automatic plan's benefits really warrant the costs entailed in getting it passed. Thus, critics argue, constitutional amendments are desirable only when some really fundamental issue is at stake, which they do not think is the case with the automatic plan. Some critics of the plan favor basing the presidential election outcome entirely on the direct vote of the citizenry. Others, however, are less concerned with possible discrepancies between electoral and popular votes than with the implications of the general-ticket system. Accordingly, they would continue to allocate electoral votes to the states but propose dividing the votes according to party voting strength within the states. The measures they advocate—the district plan and the proportional plan—lack the support thoroughgoing reformers give to the direct-vote plan and the consensus of support for the basically technical changes proposed in the automatic plan. Nonetheless, the district and proportional plans are two distinct methods that have been devised for selecting the President; and they have had significant backing over the years. They thus deserve the careful attention of those concerned with the debate on electoral reform.

☆

Chapter Six

☆

THE DISTRICT PLAN

THE PRESIDENTIAL ELECTION SYSTEM preferred by conservatives, the district plan, would eliminate the general-ticket system, which they believe favors liberals. Votes would be aggregated within local and state electoral districts in a pattern not unlike—and, under one proposal, precisely like—the allocation of House and Senate seats. As a result, the district plan would turn attention in presidential politics away from the major metropolitan areas of the most populous states.

The leading constitutional amendment[1] now pending in Congress that would institute the district plan was introduced by Senator Karl Mundt, Republican of South Dakota, in the Ninety-first Congress (1969) and in many previous years. The Mundt resolution would change the provision for allocating all of a state's electoral votes to the ticket that carries its popular votes. Instead, in the language of the resolution:

> Each state shall choose a number of electors of President and Vice President equal to the whole number of Senators and Representatives to which the state may be entitled in the Congress; but no Senator or Representative, or person holding an office of trust or profit under the United States, shall be chosen an elector.
>
> The electors assigned to each state with its Senators shall be elected by the people thereof. Each of the electors apportioned with its Rep-

1. S.J. Res. 12, in *Electing the President*, Hearings before the Subcommittee on Constitutional Amendments of the Senate Committee on the Judiciary, 91 Cong. 1 sess. (1969), pp. 636–40.

resentatives shall be elected by the people of a single-member electoral district formed by the legislature of the state. Electoral districts within each state shall be of compact and contiguous territory containing substantially equal numbers of inhabitants, and shall not be altered until another census of the United States has been taken.

Thus, in each state, two electoral votes would reflect the statewide constituency, and the remaining votes would reflect the additional single-member electoral districts. In addition, electors would be formally pledged:

Each candidate for the office of elector of President and Vice President shall file in writing under oath a declaration of the identity of the persons for whom he will vote for President and Vice President, which declaration shall be binding upon any successor to his office.

. . . Any vote cast by an elector contrary to the declaration made by him shall be counted as a vote cast in accordance with his declaration.

. . . The Congress may provide by law for the determination of questions concerning breach of faith by electors in the casting of electorla votes. . . .

The candidate who won an electoral vote majority for President would become President, and the candidate who won such a majority for Vice President would be elected to that office. Presumably, although it is not specified, both would be of the same party. If two candidates were tied, each having half the electoral votes, the candidate with a plurality of local single-elector districts—that is, of the total of district votes, excluding the two at-large votes in each state—would be declared the winner. If the electoral vote count failed to produce a winner, the election would go to Congress, where for both presidential and vice presidential contests, "the Senate and the House of Representatives together, each member having one vote, shall choose" by majority vote one of the three candidates with the most electoral votes. If there were no majority on the ballot, the choice would be narrowed to the two candidates receiving the most votes. In addition, "Congress may provide by law . . . for the case of the death of any of the persons from whom the Senate and the House of Representatives may choose a President or a Vice President whenever the right of choice shall have devolved upon them."

The Mundt district plan does not specify the local subdivisions to be established from which the electors (in addition to the two at-large electors) would be chosen. It provides only that the states shall create such districts and that they must be compact, contiguous, and relatively equal in population. The actual drawing of local district lines is left to state legislatures.

An alternative proposal that electoral votes be allocated to the states in the same way as seats in Congress was introduced in 1969 by Republican Senator Hugh Scott of Pennsylvania, the Senate minority leader.[2] The Scott plan would abolish the office of elector. Two "senatorial" electoral votes would be tallied for each state on a statewide basis; its remaining electoral votes would be aggregated within each of its House districts. The District of Columbia would also have several district electoral votes. This plan will be referred to as "the congressional district plan" to distinguish it from the Mundt plan.

Politically, any district plan would reverse the flow of forces around the presidency. The institution would be subject to a very different set of pressures than it is under the present system.

Provincial Orientation

By eliminating the general-ticket system, the district plan would significantly alter the constituency base of the presidency. It would end the preferred position of the populous states, major metropolitan areas, and their residents and substitute political advantage for the smaller states and outlying areas.

Presidential politics would be localized under the district plan. Only two of each state's electoral votes would be determined by statewide returns, except for states with additional at-large congressional jurisdictions. Essentially, there would be a newly effec-

2. S.J. Res. 25, in *ibid.*, pp. 650–56. Senator Scott had introduced similar proposals earlier.

tive political geography, the geography of local districts. Overall population would continue to be a factor; a state's size would still determine how many electoral votes it had, if any, in addition to the guaranteed minimum of three. But while 108 electoral votes would continue to be aggregated on a statewide basis—100 corresponding to each state's representation in the Senate, 5 corresponding to the present number of congressmen-at-large, and 3 from the District of Columbia—some 430 of the 538 electors (80 percent) would be chosen from local subdivisions smaller than a state.

This method of aggregating the votes would destroy the currently crucial position of the populous states by dividing their electoral votes and fragmenting their power. Accordingly, the district plan would mean a complete reversal of the existing politics of presidential elections, in which the populous states receive the most attention.

The plan would give a strategic advantage to politically homogeneous states. The most important states (as under the existing or any other system) would be those in which a party could *on balance* win the most votes. Generally, the smaller states have been less competitive politically; since they would tend to give more of their electoral votes to a single party, they would stand to benefit most under the district plan. The 1968 election offers an illustration. In that year, California recorded 40 electoral votes for Richard Nixon. Under the district plan, the situation would evidently have been different. Projections can be only tentative, because other aspects of the election contest might have been different if the electoral system had been changed. Moreover, it is impossible to say what would have happened under the Mundt plan, since the state legislatures would have drawn up the local district boundaries. Under the congressional district plan, however, if other factors had been equal, California in 1968 would have given 17 electoral votes to Hubert Humphrey and only 23 to Nixon, for a *net* Nixon advantage of 6 electoral votes. In the same election, the far less populous state of Kansas elected the Republican presidential ticket in each of its congressional districts for a gain to Nixon of 7 electoral votes. Thus, had the votes that were actually cast been tallied according to the congressional district plan, Kansas on balance would have contributed more to Nixon's margin of victory than did California, despite the fact that the Republican ticket won nearly 3 million more popular votes in California.

This comparison is no deviant case, at least when based on the actual 1968 returns under the existing system. In 1968 five or more electoral votes would have gone to the party that lost statewide in each of eight states—California, Illinois, Michigan, New Jersey, New York, Ohio, Pennsylvania, and Texas. All these states are populous and preeminent under the present system; all would lose power under the district plan. To look at the problem in another way, the states that would stand to gain strategically under the congressional district plan are those that cast all their electoral votes for the same presidential ticket. These would always include the states with only three votes, plus the most homogeneous larger states. In 1968 they would apparently have been Alabama, Alaska, Arizona, Delaware, Hawaii, Idaho, Iowa, Kansas, Louisiana, Maine, Massachusetts, Mississippi, Montana, Nebraska, Nevada, New Hampshire, New Mexico, North Dakota, Rhode Island, South Dakota, Utah, Vermont, Wyoming, and the District of Columbia. Of this group, only Massachusetts is among the most populous states today.

For similar reasons, the district plan would benefit areas lying outside the principal metropolitan centers. As the populous states' blocs of electoral votes were broken up, the leverage of their large and decisive metropolitan areas would be ended. This would correspondingly weaken the groups that, voting heavily in one direction, can now sometimes provide enough votes to swing a state into a particular party's column in November. The most any such group could do under the district plan would be to swing local districts where its members were highly concentrated and possibly two at-large electoral votes in each affected state. In the most populous state, New York, this change would mean that, instead of being able to influence forty-three electoral votes, a group could influence only a very few. Thus the interests that now provide important electoral bases for the presidency would presumably lose power. Conversely, residents of more thinly settled areas— rural and small town areas of upstate New York, New England, the Middle West, the South, the West, and so on—would evidently gain the political control over local electoral votes that they lack under the general-ticket system. And as already noted, the local votes would be more numerous than statewide votes under the district plan.

What of the suburbs? Although less celebrated than the influence of central cities in the populous states, the voting power of their suburbs is also considerable under the existing system. The district plan would end the strategic importance of populous states and their metropolitan areas, including suburbs, and give new power to nonmetropolitan areas. The impact on suburbs would vary. Suburbs in populous states and those whose interests allied them more often with core-city areas would tend to lose; suburbs in less populous states and those allied more frequently with small towns and rural areas would similarly gain.

These shifts in the constituency base of the presidency would serve to alter the policy orientation of the men holding the office. Emphasis on less populous states and areas outside the great metropolitan centers would mean that the important domestic policy influences on the President would tend to be more conservative. Also the concerns of Negroes, Jews, and similar groups with significant access under the existing system would be less influential in presidential politics under the district plan. The foreign policy orientation is harder to predict. As metropolitan areas became less salient in presidential elections, there would be less of an ethnically motivated reason for the United States to champion Israel, for example, or to take a strong stand against the Castro regime, and so on. While ethnic group pressures are by no means the sole or even the most important reason for a President's foreign policy, they are nonetheless relevant. Again, other areas would assume new importance under the district plan. The traditionally hawkish South and rural and small town areas would have a stronger hand in presidential politics.

A New Party System?

The district plan would have a wide-ranging impact on the political party system. The most important changes would result from the new local emphasis.

"Spoiler" minor parties or candidacies would be encouraged by the district plan. It is easier to campaign successfully in a few local districts than throughout an entire state or a nation. While their hopes of winning the presidency would still be scant, these parties could reasonably try to win enough local districts to throw the election into Congress more frequently. This leverage would enable "spoilers" to extract concessions from the major candidates, as George Wallace threatened to do in 1968. In addition, urban minority groups, if they perceived their loss in influence over presidential elections under the district plan, might try to regain attention in this way. And with the abolition of the general-ticket system, minor parties would probably win more electoral votes. If the actual 1968 returns had been counted by congressional districts, Wallace would have received 58 electoral votes instead of 45—an improvement of nearly 30 percent. Had the contest actually been held under district plan rules, Wallace would probably have done even better.

The use of unpledged electors as an alternative to a minor party would be eliminated by the district plan. Under the Mundt scheme, unpledged and disloyal electors would be specifically banned. Under the Scott congressional district plan, there would be no electors at all.

Increased minor party strength would tend to make the major parties less heterogeneous. Presumably, policy disagreements would be the original reason for minor party activity. Sectional diversity in the Democratic party, for example, would also decline if, as seems plausible, the rebel South split away.

In terms of party organization, local leaders would become the kingpins under the district system. Votes from their territory would specifically determine statewide and nationwide outcomes. Because of this power base, they would have a greater voice in important national party decisions. More power would accrue to the many kinds of veto groups and individuals influential in local politics. This pattern would mean that the internal structure of the parties—already local in orientation—had become more like the power structure of Congress.

How would the district system affect party competition? Proponents of the plan contend that it would increase competition, since it would do away with the general-ticket system. At the state level, the district plan would tend to split the electoral vote between or among parties. The crucial arena, however, would be the local district. Would its races be closer or more one-sided? It is hard to say without knowing the precise political units to be used. But most congressional districts are not competitive; they usually support one party with great consistency. Politicians have a propensity to draw boundaries to suit their own advantage. Even with the safeguards provided by national standards, departures from uniformity persist in state legislative districting. We foresee relatively few competitive districts under the plan.

The district plan would vastly affect the presidential nominating and campaign processes. No longer would it be as desirable that candidates come from populous states with large electoral vote blocs, or that campaigns emphasize such areas. Instead, candidates would be chosen and campaigns would be organized to appeal to the newly strategic areas—the less populated, more homogeneous states, and the areas outside the major metropolitan centers. The more homogeneous districts would take on the strategic importance the solid South once had for the Democratic party.

As the parties are presently constituted, the whole political thrust of the district plan would appear to aid the Republicans. The decline in influence of the populous states, their major metropolitan areas, minority groups, and allied forces would weaken the influence of the voters among whom Democrats are strongest— and who are strongest within the Democratic party. Forces representing interests outside the major metropolitan centers in populous states would have a new strategic importance within both major parties under the district plan.

Adoption of the district plan would probably not affect the voting behavior of citizens. Parties, candidates, and issues would continue to determine voting decisions. Attachment to the major parties might decline over time, as spoilers and other minor party candidates persistently attracted votes. A particularly popular elector might in rare instances affect a vote under the Mundt plan.

Because each voter would participate in the choice of three presidential electors, the infamous discrepancy in relative voting power between New Yorkers and Alaskans would be ended, or at least drastically reduced. Yet some districts would still be "more equal" than others. Politicians would doubtless continue to concentrate their efforts where they thought they would do the most good; and residents of those areas could accordingly get the most direct attention. Only the location of the target areas would be different.

Proponents of the district plan frequently point out that it would eliminate "wasting" votes for losing candidates at the state level; they argue that this would end the frustrations of minority party voters. However, the district plan would simply transfer the winner-take-all system, except for at-large votes, from the statewide to the local electoral district level. Except for the politicians who are responsible for getting out the vote, the disappointment of losing is caused by defeat in the election and not by the details of results within specific jurisdictions.

District plan supporters claim further that shifting the winner-take-all principle to the local level would boost the spirits of minority party voters and encourage more of them to go to the polls.

Such claims are exaggerated. Human voting motivations are complex, involving both what has been termed the "sense of political efficacy"—the belief that one's efforts make some difference—and the "sense of citizen duty"—the belief that one ought to be politically active in order to be a good citizen.[3] Changes in the voting power of certain areas might affect the sense of political efficacy of their residents, but not their sense of citizen duty.

A Circumscribed Presidency

The district plan, in our opinion, would increase the chance of electing a runner-up President. Each state would maintain two at-large electoral votes; the new single-member electoral districts would have one vote each; the overall electoral vote result would not necessarily reflect the nationwide popular vote very accurately. In 1960, for example, Richard M. Nixon would apparently have defeated John F. Kennedy in electoral votes had the congressional district plan been in effect.[4] Other presidential elections since 1952 would have produced the same winners had the votes actually cast been tallied according to congressional district plan procedures. Of course, these calculations assume that under the district plan all other things would have been equal; but they obviously would not have been equal, and so the comparison can be only broadly illustrative. It is unlikely, however, that under the Mundt plan in 1960 Kennedy would have received, as he actually did under the existing system, 303 electoral votes to 219 for Nixon. It is almost certain that the electoral college vote would have been closer, and it is possible that Nixon would have won.

3. Angus Campbell and others, *The American Voter* (John Wiley & Sons, 1960), pp. 103–07.

4. According to Neal R. Peirce, the outcome of counting the votes in 1960 by congressional district units would have been: Nixon, 278 electoral votes; Kennedy, 245 electoral votes; and 14 electoral votes for unpledged electors in the South. *The People's President* (Simon & Schuster, 1968), p. 359. American Bar Association figures give Nixon 280 and Kennedy 254. *Election of the President*, Hearings before the Senate Committee on the Judiciary, 89 Cong. 2 sess. and 90 Cong. 1 sess. (1968), pp. 124–25.

Abolishing the general-ticket system would eliminate the rapid, clear-cut victories that result when the victor's margin in the popular vote is expanded in the electoral college. During the twentieth century the popular winner has always received a greater margin in electoral than in popular votes. But, as the 1960 figures indicate, the district plan would change this pattern and sometimes even work in precisely the opposite direction. Thus, it has been estimated that if the votes actually cast had been aggregated by the rules of the congressional district plan, Presidents Eisenhower, Johnson, and Nixon would all have received fewer electoral votes in the elections that they won than they did under the existing system. Each still would have won, however.[5] Hence it appears that under the district plan the results of the electoral vote would be closer. Perhaps majorities would become less common, and more elections would go to Congress. If so, the electoral foundation of the presidency would thereby be seriously undermined.

Under the present system the possibility of prolonged indecision in a presidential election is remote; the district plan might make it more likely in certain circumstances. Also, lack of an electoral vote majority appears to us to be more likely under the district plan, which tends to deflate the winner's margin. Moreover, the district plan, by ending the general-ticket system, might mean more electoral votes for minor parties and thus an increased possibility of no electoral vote majority. Failure to produce a quick majority in the contingency election would also be possible. However, once the contest had gone that far, a joint session of Congress voting as individuals would probably produce a majority promptly, particularly under the Mundt plan provision that if the first ballot

---

5. The Peirce figures are as follows: in 1952 Eisenhower would have received 375 electoral votes under the district plan; he actually won 442. In 1956 he would have received 411 instead of 457. In 1964 Johnson would have won 466 electoral votes instead of 486. However, in each case the candidate who won under the existing system would also have won under the district plan. Peirce, *loc. cit.* In 1968 Nixon would have won with 288 electoral votes (he actually received 301) to 192 for Hubert Humphrey and 58 for George Wallace. *Congressional Quarterly Weekly Report*, Vol. 28 (June 6, 1969), pp. 885–921.

were inconclusive, the choice would be narrowed to two candidates. The Scott plan would reduce the field to the two leading candidates after the fourth ballot.

While the district plan would eliminate some conceivable sources of political instability inherent in the traditionally stable existing system, it would create potential dangers of greater magnitude. The plan would deal with problems arising from the death of candidates and electors, and it would simplify the contingency election procedure. However, under the district plan the possibility of a runner-up President would be greater. Longer periods of doubt about the election outcome would be likely. Either could cause serious disruption.

The effect on close elections would be particularly crucial. Ending the general-ticket system would tend to produce more such elections. Tallying the votes would take longer. More recounts might be demanded. With each local district controlling its own electoral vote, there would be more election officials to be tempted to tamper with returns. Prolonged deliberations during crucial periods when the country was already seriously divided would further encourage unrest.

The probable impact of the district plan on political parties presents still another threat to stability. It seems likely to us that the district plan would increase the popular and electoral vote strength of minor parties. If metropolitan minority groups felt that the presidential candidates were not very responsive to their interests and accordingly stepped up organized protests, the threat of disruption could be serious.

The new set of forces at work in electing the President would directly affect his execution of the office. The President and Congress would be elected by constituencies that under the Mundt plan would be quite similar and under the congressional district plan would be virtually identical. The political interests to which the President would be responsible under the district plan would be much more like those to which Congress as a whole is responsible today. Accordingly, the behavior of Presidents under such a system would probably be much more like the behavior of Congress. Each district would have one vote; for a President testing its political winds, the most reliable indicator would presumably be the inclinations of its congressman. Congress and the President would not be exactly alike even under the congressional district plan, because of differing interests, attitudes, and perceptions and because the President is one individual and Congress is a collegial body with unequal distributions of power among its members. But clearly they would have reason to be more nearly alike.

The extreme case of similarity between President and Congress would occur if Congress began electing the President more frequently because there was no electoral vote majority. The congressional district plan in elections since 1952 would apparently have reduced each winner's margin of electoral victory, and indeed in 1960 would have turned the Kennedy victory into defeat. Thus, the district plan might send more contingency elections to Congress. Obviously the power of the legislative branch would thereby be enormously enhanced.

In our opinion, the localization of the President's constituency that would occur under the district plan would weaken the presidency. While everyone knows today that the President is not really the choice of all the people or of all the voters or even of all those who cast ballots in the states he carries, he appears to be something more than master of a coalition of petty sovereignties. For all the local touches of a campaign—"What did Dick Nixon ever do for Culpeper?" Lyndon Johnson is reported to have asked at a Virginia whistlestop in 1960—it is essentially geared to the United States as a nation. Candidates make extensive use of the national mass media. The strategic importance of various areas under the existing electoral system is not ignored; the candidates' principal public appearances usually take place within the major metropolitan centers of populous states. On the campaign trail, a candidate typically makes brief obeisance to the locality and state in which he is speaking and then emphasizes the main points of his national campaign. Once in office, Presidents still operate within a political world where they must continuously weigh the political costs and benefits of contemplated actions in the nice balance of a ward heeler's scale; but the national interest weighs increasingly heavily with the importance of the issue being considered.

Under the district plan, presidential candidates and Presidents would have to be concerned with the parochial politics of the 538 electoral districts. Some 430 of the 538 electoral votes would be aggregated on the basis of smaller local districts rather than on a statewide basis. And fewer Americans now live and will live in the sparsely settled states that would become much more important under the district plan than in the populous states that are powerful under the existing system. How would Presidents and would-be Presidents cope with this shift? No one can be certain. In our opinion, national campaigns, national appeals, and concern with the national interest would not disappear. The presidency would still be the apex of the American political system. But regardless of his actions the President would tend to appear—like the new plan for electing him—more parochial. Every four years the public would hear commentators announce the popular vote returns, explain the electoral system, and attempt to aggregate the votes by districts. Though the popular vote winner would probably win, a close election would appear to be hanging on a few ballots in obscure localities. Every ten years the results of the census would be published, electoral votes would be reallocated, and states gaining or losing votes would have to redistrict; others might also. Usually the incumbent President would have considerable interest in the outcome; but he would have Hobson's choice of intervening and being denounced for tampering with the electoral system, or not intervening and leaving himself at the mercy of local politicians. These developments would not enhance the prestige of the presidency.

The Critical Power of State Legislatures

No powers would flow directly from the national government to the state governments, or vice versa, as a result of the district plan. However, the state legislatures would become the scene of important contests in the establishment of electoral district boundaries between metropolitan and nonmetropolitan areas, between Democrats and Republicans, and among other factions.

At present, the federal Constitution authorizes the state legislatures to direct how electors are to be selected. Under the district plan, the Constitution would require state legislators to establish district lines within their jurisdictions. The general-ticket system is a virtually universal rule today; the district system would be universal under the district plan. Thus, in the method of aggregating the votes, no significant shift in the balance of national and state powers would be involved. Similarly, the states would also maintain their responsibility for election administration under the district plan, in the context of federal voting rights guarantees.

Setting up electoral districts, however, would generate political conflict; and the state legislatures would be the arena for resolving them. The Mundt plan would establish federal standards requiring that districts be compact, contiguous, and relatively equal in population. The number of local districts would still have to be equal to each state's congressional representation and would thus be subject to reassessment after each decennial census. Otherwise, states would be free to establish whatever kinds of local districts they wanted.

Drawing congressional district lines, already a power of the state legislatures, would become doubly important under the Scott plan. Some critics have argued that giving the states the power to determine electoral district boundaries would make gerrymandering inevitable. This condemns all state legislatures out of hand. However, legislatures would be allowed wide leeway, and it is unreasonable to expect that elected officials would make public policy decisions on a wholly apolitical basis. Moreover, the physical and political geography of the American states is such that they cannot readily be divided into neat, standardized districts. Unless the strength of all parties were evenly distributed throughout each state, any district lines, however fastidiously drawn, would help some factions and hurt others. There is rarely, if ever, such a distribution of party strength.

A Fundamental Reconstruction of the Presidency

The basic premise underlying the district plan is that a new constituency for Presidents should be created—a constituency more local than national in base. The plan is actually one of many designed to "bring the government back home to the people." Obviously, the government—the presidency in this case—already belongs to the voters or, more precisely, to those who cast a plurality of the popular votes aggregated by states. Nor would the district plan initiate any real local control over the way in which a President governed. The proposed plan would instead mean using local districts to aggregate the votes. Proponents of the district plan think that the political forces they favor stand the greatest chance of success in the local districts. And the local districts also provide the constituency base of Congress—the national institution with which they are in greatest sympathy.

The district plan must be considered to be more than a remedy for supposed defects of the electoral college system. It is really a protest against the sort of presidency that has developed during the twentieth century. Advocates of the plan seek to overturn policies they oppose and balances of power unfavorable to them by recasting the popular base of the presidential office. This is an entirely legitimate way to seek to effect change in the American system. But it should be understood that to support the district plan is to endorse a profound political reversal.

☆

Chapter Seven

☆

THE PROPORTIONAL PLAN

LIKE THE DISTRICT PLAN, the proportional plan would continue the state electoral vote system but end the general-ticket system. While the district plan would divide state electoral votes by smaller districts, however, the proportional plan would divide them by the popular vote received by each political party. As in the case of the district plan and the direct-vote plan, the proportional plan would have political effects very different from those of the existing system. Notably, it would bring an end to the two-party norm, the metropolitan orientation, and the solid presidential mandate of the present presidential election process.

The principal proportional plan of the Ninety-first Congress was introduced in January 1969 by Democratic Senator Sam J. Ervin, Jr., of North Carolina. Essentially similar to the Lodge-Gossett proposal considered by Congress in the 1950s, the Ervin amendment[1] would abolish the electoral college and the office of elector. Instead, "the President and Vice President shall be elected by the people of the several states and the District [of Columbia]." The administration of elections would remain a state matter, "but the Congress may at any time by law make or alter" state regulations. Electoral votes would be allocated to the states and the District on the same basis as at present. However, within each state, electoral

1. S.J. Res. 2, in *Electing the President*, Hearings before the Subcommittee on Constitutional Amendments of the Senate Committee on the Judiciary, 91 Cong. 1 sess., pp. 626–30.

votes would be divided proportionately by party. In the language of the proposed amendment:

> Each person for whom votes were cast for President in each State and such district [of Columbia] shall be credited with such proportion of the electoral votes thereof as he received of the total vote of the electors [voters] therein for President. In making the computation, fractional numbers less than one one-thousandth shall be disregarded. The person having the greatest number of electoral votes for President shall be President if such number be at least 40 percentum of the whole number of such electoral votes. If no person has received at least 40 percentum of the whole number of electoral votes, or if two persons have received an identical number of electoral votes which is at least 40 percentum of the whole ... then from the persons having the two greatest numbers of electoral votes for President, the Senate and the House of Representatives sitting in joint session shall choose immediately, by ballot, the President. A majority of the votes of the combined authorized membership of the Senate and the House of Representatives shall be necessary for a choice.
>
> The Vice President shall be likewise elected. . . .

The amendment also empowers Congress to pass legislation to deal with the possible death of a candidate.

A compromise plan[2] introduced by Senator Hubert H. Humphrey of Minnesota in 1956 suggested a variation on the proportional theme. Each state would be allocated two electoral votes to be cast for the presidential ticket with the most popular votes statewide. The remaining electoral votes would be divided proportionately according to the nationwide popular vote totals of each presidential slate. In essence, this proposal in substance and in political implications was an amalgam of the Lodge-Gossett plan and of the direct-vote plan that Humphrey had supported in other years.

Another kind of proportional plan was introduced in the House in 1969 by Republican Representative Frank Horton of New

---

2. S.J. Res. 152, 84 Cong. 2 sess. (1954), described in Ralph M. Goldman, "A New Proposal for Electoral College Reform," *Midwest Journal of Political Science*, Vol. 2 (February 1958), pp. 89–96.

York.[3] This measure would abolish each state's at-large electoral votes, allocate electoral votes on the basis of representation in the House alone, and divide them in proportion to the statewide popular vote. Electoral votes would thus conform more closely to state population and state voter turnout. This plan would also be a compromise between the Lodge-Gossett plan and the direct-vote plan in its effects. It has not aroused much political support.

When electoral college reform received a test in the Senate in 1956, the key vote came on a measure that would have allowed each state to choose between the district plan and the proportional plan. The proposal was another unsuccessful effort at compromise. Clearly, such a system would have been difficult for officials to administer and for citizens to comprehend. State power would have been enhanced. Otherwise, its effects would have been those of the district and proportional plans in some unpredictable combination, depending on what the states decided to do.

The proportional plan is aimed principally at two aspects of the present electoral system: the electoral college, with its possibly independent-minded electors, and the general-ticket system, with its statewide winner-take-all principle. Advocates of the proportional plan also say their plan would make the electoral vote outcome more closely reflect the popular vote.

Less obvious, and little discussed, are the plan's political implications. This disregard of political consequences characterizes the electoral reform debate generally; but the proportional plan is a special case. Many critics of the old Lodge-Gossett plan charged that it would encourage a multiparty system, perhaps proportional representation in Congress, and even parliamentary government. These assertions were overstatements. The tendency of the plan to check severely the existing power of major metropolitan areas in presidential elections is more important and has been generally overlooked.

3. H.J. Res. 345, in *Electoral College Reform*, Hearings before the House Committee on the Judiciary, 91 Cong. 1 sess. (1969), pp. 841–45.

The New Strategic Advantage of "Safe" Areas

The leading metropolitan centers of the most populous states would lose their political leverage under the proportional plan, just as they would under the direct-vote plan, the district plan, or any other plan that eliminated the general-ticket system. As with the two plans previously discussed, the proportional scheme would shift the advantage to those areas that produced large pluralities for a presidential ticket.

The states that are of moderate size and are most politically homogeneous would tend to have the largest margins of electoral vote victory under the proportional plan. These politically "safe" states have usually, although not always, been more sparsely populated than the states that are powerful under the existing system. For example, if the popular votes actually cast in the 1960 election had been tallied according to the proportional plan, assuming that other factors were constant, the only states that would have yielded the winning candidate a margin of at least 1.5 electoral votes over his nearest competitor would have been Georgia, Kansas, Louisiana, Massachusetts, New York, and Ohio. In 1968 this list would have named Alabama, the District of Columbia, Georgia, Indiana, Louisiana, Massachusetts, Mississippi, and New York.[4] Only three of these states—Massachusetts, New York, and Ohio—are among the eleven most populous and powerful states under the existing presidential electoral system. Under the proportional plan, the internal solidarity of the states cited would have made them greater political prizes. By the same token, states in which competition is very keen, whether they are populous or not, would have been of less importance.

A dramatic illustration of this pattern is the shift in effective political power between Vermont and New York. If each state's electoral votes in 1960 had been tallied according to proportional

4. *Ibid.*, pp. 976–81.

rules, Richard M. Nixon would have received 1.759 of Vermont's
3 electoral votes and John F. Kennedy, 1.240, giving Nixon a
margin of 0.519. In New York, Kennedy would have won 22.700
of the state's electoral votes and Nixon, the remaining 22.300; the
result would have been a Kennedy margin of 0.400 in the Empire
State.[5] While the rewards of getting out the vote in New York
would have been greater in absolute terms, the margin of victory
would have been greater in Vermont. Thus a small homogeneous
state could yield more to a winner than a large competitive state.
The greatest prize, of course, would be to win a large state by a
large margin. However, most of the more populous states are very
competitive politically.

Correspondingly, the metropolitan areas of the most populous
states would lose the potential power they now have under the
general-ticket system to swing all of the state's bloc of electoral
votes. As a result, all other areas would stand to gain. While the
new premium on partisan homogeneity might benefit some solidly
Democratic big-city wards, the major beneficiaries would be one-
party small town, rural, and suburban areas outside the populous
states. The politically competitive areas would become less important because the electoral effect within a state of their popular
voting patterns would be in effect a standoff.

This decline of the metropolitan centers has obvious policy implications, in a conservative direction. The effect on the two major
parties would be somewhat different. Almost certainly, the Republican orientation in presidential elections would be changed; the
Democratic case is more complicated.

The Republican party's base in recent decades has been strongest
in the Midwest and Far West and, increasingly, the South; but its
presidential candidates have been oriented to a considerable degree
by the existing electoral vote system in the same direction as the
Democratic nominees—toward metropolitan areas and populous
states. Though the Republican party is surely the more conserva-

5. This comparison was suggested by Professor Ruth C. Silva.

tive on social welfare issues, its candidates too have had to appeal to liberal-tending residents of metropolitan areas if they hoped to win. With an end to the state general-ticket system under the proportional plan, the more solidly Republican—and more conservative—states would be more powerful within the party. Thus we think it likely that, under the proportional plan, the Republicans would tend to nominate for President someone who is conservative on social welfare, less attuned to minority group concerns, and possibly less internationalist than most of their candidates have been in the past.

By placing a premium on winning large pluralities, the proportional plan would mean some continued influence for the big cities within the Democratic party. Core-city areas and the Democratic party in states where such areas predominate would still encourage the presidential party to be liberal on domestic welfare issues, oriented toward the policy interests of key urban groups, and at least cautiously internationalist as well.

Yet we have seen that smaller, less populous states would assume a new strategic importance under the proportional plan because they are more politically homogeneous and thus produce a larger margin of victory. For this reason, Democrats might be inclined to make more appeals to these states and even to their nonmetropolitan areas. Any such appeals would tend to be less social-welfare oriented than the party line traditionally followed in wooing urban voters.

Turnabout in the Party System

Most discussion of the proportional plan has concerned its putative effects on the parties. In particular, its propensity to encourage a multiparty system has been widely emphasized. Clearly, adoption of the proportional plan would mean a considerable change in the position of minor parties, internal party structure, the amount of interparty competition, and the nomination and campaign processes.

To what extent would the proportional plan affect the two-party tradition? It would tend to improve the fortunes of minor parties. Under the existing system, they have been electorally influential primarily at the state and local level, either by swinging an election to or from a major party candidate or by carrying a few states. But on a nationwide scale the minor parties have ultimately failed because of the general-ticket system; their popular vote percentage has almost inevitably been greater than their electoral vote percentage. Under the proportional plan, in contrast, the strength of minor parties would be reflected on a statewide basis. Thus, local minor parties like the New York Liberals would stand to lose their swing vote power in presidential elections; but national minor parties like those of Henry Wallace and, potentially, George Wallace might gain. Certainly "spoiler" candidacies would be encouraged. Not only would their votes "count"; they might determine whether any candidate won the necessary 40-percent plurality. If they were successful, other groups dissatisfied with the major parties—perhaps urban minority groups who thought that they had inadequate influence within those parties—might find it advantageous to mount additional minor party candidacies as a way of demonstrating their national strength. This pattern would be similar to that anticipated under the direct-vote plan.

Party differences would sharpen. With no more opportunity to run unpledged electors, rebel Democrats seeking to protest their national party policies and leadership would have to conform or join another party. Minor parties would be encouraged. Probably over time a realignment of parties on broad policy grounds would take place. Notably, extremist factions would leave the major parties.

The proportional plan would remodel the power structure within the parties. It would no longer be relevant, for example, that a leader could influence enough votes to carry his state for the party; what would matter would be his ability to produce the largest possible percentage of as many electoral votes as possible. This system would reward the local and state leaders who controlled the politically homogeneous areas.

Competition between or among parties within the states would be increased under the proportional plan. Any plan that ended the general-ticket system would do that. There are no longer any truly one-party states, as there still were when the Lodge-Gossett proposal was made in the 1950s. Nonetheless, the proportional plan would provide greater incentive for all parties to campaign vigorously; each state's electoral votes would be divided proportionately according to the popular vote, instead of being awarded as a group to the party that finished first. In addition, the proportional plan would put a premium on states where a dominant party could roll up larger margins of victory. As a result, parties other than the most dominant could be expected to fight hard to prevent its gaining such an advantage. Both the proportional division and the importance of the margin of victory would tend to boost party competition.

Adoption of the proportional plan would also reconstruct the politics of the nominating process. Because state electoral votes would be divided and smaller, the more homogeneous states would become more powerful, and there would be less incentive to select presidential and vice presidential nominees from large, doubtful states. To be sure, a party might choose such a man in the belief that he could win many votes in his home state; but it could no longer hope that he could carry all its electoral votes. Probably many candidates from populous states would continue to be nominated; but logically, candidates from other states would have a better chance.

The effect on campaign strategy would be the same. With the abolition of the state general-ticket system, the more competitive populous states would no longer provide large blocs of electoral votes to the ticket that carried them; accordingly, they would decline in relative importance. More homogeneous states, including smaller states, would arouse new interest. Candidates would no longer need to concentrate on populous states and their leading metropolitan areas; the rest of the country would receive more attention. As this geographic emphasis shifted, so would the location of the voters who had an opportunity to see presidential candidates in person. Much campaigning would continue to be done on television and radio. But much of each party's total resources for direct campaigning would be expended where its prospects looked best. There would be more preaching to the converted, which would minimize any educational benefits of campaigning.

At the same time, the minority party or parties within each state, including rank-and-file members and sympathizers, would be revitalized. With the prospect of receiving a substantial proportion of the state's electoral votes, minority party workers who had seen their efforts go for naught every four years would at last see them "count." But they would probably receive short shrift from national party campaign strategists, who would be concentrating on sure states where there were the most electoral votes to gain. Nonetheless, local minority party leaders would certainly be encouraged to try harder.

Thus, under the proportional plan, some citizens would continue to be "more equal" than others in terms of presidential campaigns. Only the relative direction of advantage and disadvantage would shift.

Still, the proportional plan might mean some decline in apathy. We have noted earlier the distinction between public indifference based on a lack of a sense of political efficacy and that resulting from a lack of a sense of citizen duty. Clearly the latter is harder to change. However, proponents of the proportional plan imply that the former would be alleviated in some degree by encouraging those minority party voters who previously had felt that their votes did not count.

If the two major parties remained predominant and continued to command their traditional loyalties, or if minor party movements drew equally from the major parties, the proportional plan would serve Republican interests. The Republicans would immediately gain from the decline in the influence of populous states and their metropolitan centers. These areas, on balance, have been the cornerstone of Democratic strength in presidential campaigns. The Republicans have had superior strength in the countryside.

The evidence is mixed on whether Republicans would benefit from a proportional count of their recent gains in the South. Until the Eisenhower elections, states below the Mason-Dixon line were solidly Democratic. But Eisenhower carried four states of the old Confederacy in 1952 and five in 1956. Richard Nixon in 1960 captured 33 electoral votes in three southern states. Had the votes actually cast in 1960 been tallied according to the proportional plan, Nixon would have received 56.872 southern electoral votes. Barry Goldwater, who won only about one-third of the popular vote nationwide, received 47 electoral votes in Alabama, Georgia, Louisiana, Mississippi, and South Carolina. Aggregating the votes actually cast in 1964 under the rules of the proportional plan would have given Goldwater 64.629 southern electoral votes. However, in 1968, perhaps because of George Wallace's candidacy, the Democrats rather than the Republicans would have gained in the South if electoral votes had been counted by the proportional method. The Democratic ticket actually received 25 southern electoral votes; under the proportional plan, if other factors had been constant, it would have received 39.136 electoral votes. The Republicans, who actually won 57 southern electoral votes, would have won only 43.312 under the proportional plan.[6]

In short, the South is no longer a Democratic stronghold. But it does not have a mature two-party system. In Chapter 5 we expressed our expectation that the South, after a gradual realignment, will have a two-party system in this generation. In light of national trends, we believe that southern conservatives will eventually ally with the national Republicans and southern liberals with the Democrats. Some scholars foresee three parties—Democrats, Republicans, and Dixiecrats—in the South even under the existing system. We consider the two-party pattern more likely under the present system; the proportional plan would encourage minor parties.

The Democrats would suffer serious losses under the propor-

6. These illustrative figures are derived from the *Hearings* cited in note 3, above, pp. 976–81.

tional plan. They would tend to gain electoral votes where they are usually the second strongest party—in upper New England, the rural Midwest, and the Far West. In time the proportional plan might even serve Democratic interests in the South. However, these gains would hardly compensate for the loss of the opportunity the Democrats now have to win principally by carrying competitive, populous states by narrow margins.

In terms of internal party structure, the proportional plan would strengthen the most loyal states that produce the most votes for a party. During the 1950s, many proponents and opponents alike of the Lodge-Gossett plan believed that it would benefit southern Democrats within their party. In the 1970s it would not. Also, some formerly rock-ribbed Republican areas in New England and in some states west of the Mississippi have become more politically competitive. There are still many safe congressional districts, but very few consistently safe states. To the degree that safe areas continued to adhere to their traditions of returning landslide majorities for the winning party, their political leaders would have a strong role within the councils of that party.

The Problem of Presidential Legitimacy

We think that the proportional plan could create a crisis in presidential legitimacy. Of course, this is often said of the existing system by critics who point out that it could theoretically produce a runner-up President. We have already discussed why we believe such an eventuality is extremely unlikely under the present system. However, the election of a runner-up President does seem quite conceivable under the proportional plan. Moreover, the difficulties inherent in the vote-counting procedure, the probable threat to political stability, and the consequent effects on the President's conduct in office all bode ill for the presidency.

Although it is intended to reflect the popular vote more accurately than does the existing system, the proportional plan would distort the nationwide popular total. Each state would still have a minimum of three electoral votes. Additional electoral votes would be based on outdated population figures rather than on the actual turnout at the polls. The need to round off percentages would provide another, though minor, distortion. Thus in theory the outcome of the popular vote across the country would not necessarily be the same as the sum of the state outcomes figured under the proportional plan.

An analysis of past elections suggests how frequently a runner-up President might have been elected. If the plan had been adopted, of course, other aspects of the campaign would have been different; and so such projections can be only illustrative and not conclusive. With other factors assumed to be constant, however, it has been estimated that Samuel J. Tilden would have beaten Rutherford B. Hayes in 1876, Winfield S. Hancock would have triumphed over James A. Garfield in 1880, Grover Cleveland would have defeated Benjamin Harrison in 1888, William Jennings Bryan would have edged William McKinley in 1896, and, according to some calculations,[7] Richard M. Nixon would have won over John F. Kennedy

7. Several different counts have been made of the 1960 returns using proportional plan rules. Results differ as to how many electoral votes the Democratic and Republican tickets would have received and even as to which would have won.

There are a number of reasons for these discrepancies. One concerns the method of counting votes for unpledged electors—as votes for the Democratic ticket, or as votes for "other candidates." Another problem is the issue of how to count the Alabama vote for a slate of partly pro-Kennedy and partly unpledged electors, a controversy discussed earlier. A further point of potential difficulty is the extent of arithmetic detail: at what digit to stop counting, and whether to round off or drop the next digit altogether. Apparently in all the sources cited the Lodge-Gossett rules were used, and the fourth digit was dropped.

Neal R. Peirce, using computations made by *Congressional Quarterly*, has calculated that Nixon would have received 266.075 electoral votes and Kennedy 265.623. His figures award five-elevenths of the highest Alabama Democratic elector vote to Kennedy and six-elevenths to the unpledged slate. *The People's President*, p. 358; *Nomination and Election of President and Vice President and Qualifications for Voting*, Hearings before the Senate Committee on the Judiciary, 87 Cong. 1 sess. (1961), p. 411.

The Legislative Reference Service of the Library of Congress, in charts prepared in 1969 for the House Judiciary Committee, used the *Congressional Quarterly* data but recalculated those totals. Under the LRS arithmetic, again Nixon would have won, 263.632 to 262.671. *Electoral College Reform*, Hearings (1969), pp. 980–81.

However, under computations made by the American Bar Association and by Professor Ruth C. Silva of Pennsylvania State University, Kennedy would have won with

in 1960. These putative results would have meant the election of one candidate, Tilden, who evidently won a popular *majority* but lost in electoral votes, and of another, Cleveland, who got a popular *plurality* but ultimately lost the election. It would also have meant victory for two runner-up candidates—Hancock in 1880 and Bryan in 1896. It might also have meant victory for Nixon in the 1960 election, in which the popular vote figures were in dispute. Thus the proportional plan, while aimed at reflecting the popular vote more accurately, might sometimes do the reverse.

The proportional plan apparently would have reduced the margin of victory in nearly every presidential election from 1864 to 1968. The sole exception is in 1916, when Woodrow Wilson would have won by a wider margin.[8] In more recent times, Dwight D. Eisenhower would have received 288.5 electoral votes in 1952 according to the proportional division instead of 442; in 1956 he would have received 296.7 instead of 457; in 1960, as has been noted, John F. Kennedy would have received 260-odd instead of 303; in 1964 Lyndon B. Johnson would have received 320.0 instead of 486; and in 1968 Richard M. Nixon would have received 231.53 instead of 301.[9] These data strongly suggest that the inherent bias of the proportional plan would be the reverse of that of the existing system. Instead of inflating the President's electoral

---

266.136 electoral votes to Nixon's 263.662. The ABA figures allocate all the controversial unpledged elector votes except for three in Mississippi to the Democrats. *Election of the President*, Hearings before the Senate Committee on the Judiciary, 89 Cong. 2 sess., and 90 Cong. 1 sess. (1968), p. 125. Professor Silva supplied her unpublished figures to the authors.

One of the principal lessons for a student of these numbers is the dubious reliability of projecting the outcome of past elections run under one electoral system by the hypothetical rules of another. Obviously, if the 1960 race had actually been run under the proportional plan, there would have been two separate slates—or at least one consistent slate—of dissident and of national Democrats in the relevant southern states. Each method used by scholars to count the controversial votes is defensible, but neither, for reasons beyond scholarly control, is very satisfactory.

8. Peirce, *loc. cit.*

9. From tables supplied to the House Judiciary Committee by the Legislative Reference Service, printed in *Electoral College Reform*, Hearings cited in note 3, above, pp. 977–85.

majority, the plan would deflate his victory margin and along with it his decisive mandate to govern.

The proportional plan would not foster citizen understanding of, and confidence in, the vote-counting process for presidential elections. It would introduce a complex and cumbersome procedure for tallying the votes that is difficult for anyone—politician, political scientist, or ordinary citizen—to understand. The proportional plan is difficult to comprehend; it would be more difficult to follow the counting procedures as returns became available on election night. The total vote in each state would have to be established before final counts could be made. In some elections the winner's identity would not be clear to the public until every vote was in in every state and until state-by-state calculations had been made of each candidate's percentage (to three decimal points, with the fourth disregarded) of electoral votes determined by the final popular tally. A complex arithmetic formula would in effect be written into the Constitution. Commentators and schoolboys who complain about the complications of the electoral college system today would have far more to contend with under the proportional plan.

Because of the intricacies of the vote-counting process under the proportional plan, an extended period of doubt about the election result would no longer be only a remote possibility; it would be a common pattern. It would take longer to tally the vote. The tally system would be far more difficult to explain than the electoral college system. (There are at least three different counts, all from usually very reliable sources, of the 1960 returns using the proportional rules. Popular votes for unpledged electors present the major problem in making the tally.) Recounts might well be more frequent. This process would hardly ensure enhanced political stability.

There are further reasons why the plan would have an unsettling effect. While the current proportional plan amendment would remove problems connected with electors and would give Congress formal authority to act in case of the death of a candidate, these have not been serious threats to the smooth operation of the political system; and some aspects of the proportional plan would entail such threats. Besides the cumbersome vote-counting procedure, the plan would tend to make elections more close. The President would no longer have an inflated electoral majority based on the state general-ticket system. Indeed, he might have a very narrow base of support. Because of increased minor party activity, Presidents would be elected with between 40 and 50 percent of the popular vote; more elections might have to go to Congress for final determination. Such narrow victories would emphasize national division rather than national unity.

In particular, increased division might mean more political ferment if disaffected groups, notably Negro groups, were further disillusioned by the dilution of their current voting strength. It is difficult for us to say whether a substantial number of those affected would perceive a change in the mechanics of presidential elections in this way; it is equally difficult to say whether such perception would seriously disrupt the political system. But certainly a diminution of urban power in selecting the chief political officer in the United States would not please city dwellers, who already think that their home areas have been callously neglected for too long. We need not detail what the chronic and extreme alienation of these groups could mean for the political order.

We believe that a President elected in such circumstances would from the outset have difficulty in governing; difficulties of all sorts tend to increase throughout any chief executive's fixed four-year term. Eliminating the expanded electoral margin given the President under the existing system, increasing the possibility of a runner-up President, taking longer to decide, emphasizing divisions in the electorate—all these trends would mean that a President who won in a close election would begin with a poor power position in the Washington community. And it is in the close contests that the nature of the electoral system becomes important; in the one-sided contests, everyone concedes the identity of the rightful winner.[10] Under no electoral system would the 1936 or

10. A possible indirect effect that has been frequently discussed is that use of the proportional plan to elect the President might encourage use of proportional represen-

1964 outcomes have been disputed; however, under some systems the 1960 or 1968 results might have been.

Federalism Unchanged

The one major aspect of presidential politics that would not be changed by the proportional plan is the sharing of powers by the national and state governments. The state would continue to be the unit within which electoral votes were aggregated. Of course, state legislatures would lose their power to choose the form of electoral system used within their boundaries, but this power is not very significant. Again, though the state governments would initially maintain control over the administration of elections, Congress would specifically be granted standby powers to establish national standards; even if this clause were not adopted, Congress could enact such standards. In the current policy debate, advocates of the proportional plan have contended that it is the only electoral reform measure that would preserve the existing national-state relationship and at the same time reflect the popular vote outcome more closely. They are correct about the federal system but wrong in saying that the plan would assure victory to the popular vote winner.

Otherwise, the proportional plan has much in common with both the district plan and the direct-vote plan; all would abolish the state general-ticket system. From that change stem the major implications of all three proposed plans: undermining the two-party tradition, curbing the strength of the metropolitan areas, and weakening the presidential mandate to govern. Each of the three, however, would provide a unique constituency for the President. The Lodge-Gossett plan, like the district plan, was aimed specifically at the presumed power of the big cities. While it resembles the district plan in that respect, however, the proportional

---

tation (P.R.) in electing members of Congress. There is no direct relationship between the two ideas. No plural executive would be created by the proportional plan. Moreover, proportional representation is very unfashionable in the United States. A change to P.R. in this country hardly seems likely, particularly a change solely because of a change in the presidential election system.

plan does not share the district plan's extreme local emphasis. Instead, the proportional plan, like the direct-vote plan, would mean encouragement of nationwide minority-strength factions. The middle position of the proportional plan thus appealed during the 1950s both to conservatives who objected to the metropolitan bias of the existing system, and to progressives who were concerned with the antidemocratic idea of the electoral college. Perhaps the Lodge-Gossett plan failed because some supporters on both sides detected its ambivalence. At present, most conservatives have retreated to the district plan, and most of those concerned with ensuring that the President elected be the winner of the popular vote prefer to go all the way to the direct-vote plan. The chief political problem of the proportional plan thus appears to be that it does not really satisfy any significant group.

☆

Chapter Eight

☆

CONCLUSIONS AND RECOMMENDATIONS

OVER ALMOST TWO CENTURIES, Americans have devised a variety of possible ways to choose their Chief Executive. The electoral system established by the founding fathers was born in some controversy and has been the object of periodic criticism ever since. In recent decades four main substitutes—the direct-vote plan, the automatic plan, the district plan, and the proportional plan—have been seriously considered; but no constitutional change has been made. At stake are issues both of political theory and of practical politics. The public debate has usually not been very spirited; there has been little consideration of the likely political effects of reform. Each of the plans has been shown to have both merits and defects.

The authors of this book conclude that the electoral vote system, with the winner-take-all, state general-ticket system, is the best of the several methods.

The Existing System

The original electoral framework has permitted political adaptations that have produced Presidents in forty-six elections. The system was last modified constitutionally in 1804, but it has constantly evolved in response to political change. Only twice, in 1800 and 1824, has the electoral college itself failed to produce a majority and thus thrown the election into the House. The present ar-

135

rangement, with the Twelfth Amendment, the general-ticket system, and the two-party system, now effectively precludes the situations that occurred in 1800 and 1824. Only once, in 1876, just a decade after the Civil War, has there been a serious disruption for other reasons. And only once, in 1888, was there a clear-cut case of the system's producing a runner-up President. We have suggested that such an occurrence is far less likely today. Because resort to the contingency election procedure has been rare and an electoral vote majority represents a solid popular mandate, the system has produced Presidents with generally accepted authority to govern for four years. Although Lord Bryce noted in 1888, with some contemporary wisdom, that great men do not become President, the quality of those elected under the present system has generally been high. From a functional standpoint, then, the system has worked well. Opponents have attacked it primarily on other grounds.

Some critics find fault with its political effects. Many are particularly dissatisfied with the state general-ticket system, by which all of a state's electoral votes go to the candidate who wins that state, however narrow his statewide plurality. Under the electoral college system in the twentieth century, residents of major metropolitan areas of the most populous states have enjoyed disproportionate power in nominating presidential candidates, received more attention in their campaigns, and thereby affected their elections and policies; residents of other areas have understandably resented the imbalance. Yet these metropolitan areas encompass many of the nation's urgent domestic problems—notably hard-core, long-term poverty, with all the social ills it implies, and environmental pollution, which threatens the health of all citizens. While they are not limited to metropolitan areas, these problems are intensified by the concentration of population in those areas. Solutions to the problems, moreover, are beyond the capacity of local jurisdictions and have long been virtually ignored by state and national legislatures, in which the metropolis is still underrepresented and unlikely ever to be predominant. The populous states are more nearly microcosms of the future nation than is any other group of states. Moreover, the political persuasions of metropolitan area residents appear to coincide with those of a majority of the nation's voters; most of the populous states have gone as the popular votes of the nation have gone in the last six elections. It is also claimed that the present system allows minority groups in the major cities to exert excessive influence on presidential policy. As crucial groups in crucial states they hold views that may be especially important to a President concerned with public opinion; but they hardly dictate policy. The groups may differ within and among themselves as to the appropriate course of action on a given issue. In addition, the President in assessing opinion must take account of attitudes outside the metropolis.

Indeed, a general distinction must be drawn between the closer attention to metropolitan needs generated by the general-ticket system under the electoral college system and the remote possibility that the leverage of metropolitan areas might make the electoral outcome different from the popular outcome. The first tendency is a matter of fact; the second is mainly speculation.

Some critics have also attacked the idea that electors may vote for someone other than the candidate chosen by the voters of their states. They have done so a few times recently. Though the infidelity of these electors has never changed the outcome of an election, it is undesirable because it contravenes the popular will as expressed at the polls. But the voters in states where this happens are not always or even usually hapless victims. The election of maverick electors may be, at least in part, a fault of the system under which they were chosen by their party as members of a ticket—presumably without sufficient dissemination or understanding of their individual views. Any remedy would thus appear to be a logical and easily met responsibility of state and local party leaders.

Unpledged electors are also criticized by those who would reform the existing system. There is no doubt that the unpledged electors of Mississippi, and probably those of Alabama, who preferred Harry F. Byrd to John F. Kennedy in 1960, did in fact reflect the views of a majority of those who chose them as electors. To say that the voters of those states should have had to choose between Kennedy and Nixon is to deny them the alternative of a third party, which is what the unpledged elector movement amounted to. The fairest arrangements, in our opinion, would have been to allow Alabama and Mississippi voters a choice among electoral slates supporting the Republicans, the national Democrats, and the dissident Democrats. The lack of an opportunity to vote for a national candidate like Johnson in Alabama in 1964 and the presence of mixed slates like the partly unpledged, partly Kennedy Democratic slate in Alabama in 1960, are both clearly undesirable because the choices of the voters cannot be adequately registered. But the remedy does not necessarily require a constitutional amendment.

Another technical aspect of the existing system that has aroused criticism is that Congress has the power to choose the President and Vice President in a contingency election if no candidate receives a majority in the electoral college. We share the critics' belief in the desirability of an independent electoral base for the President. But the contingency election procedure does not threaten this base; it does not make the President a creature of Congress. The power of the House to choose the President has not been exercised since 1825, nor the Senate's power to choose the Vice President since 1837. Furthermore, Congress has similar powers in other rare contingencies—notably under the presidential disability amendment, supported by many of those who oppose the contingency election procedure. The House vote by state delegations rather than by individuals is unduly provincial; and a rapid, clearcut choice would be facilitated by narrowing the contest from the top three to the top two candidates. However, time has shown these provisions to be of little importance in presidential elections.

The effects of the existing system on the political parties have been widely debated. For example, the power of minor parties to swing elections in states or in the electoral college has often been criticized. Yet minor parties are probably less powerful under the present electoral vote system than they would be under any of the alternatives thus far proposed. Historically, their percentage of the electoral vote has usually trailed their percentage of the popular vote. Again, some Republicans and others are opposed to the alleged recent tendency of the existing system to favor the Democrats. Far more than the electoral college is at work here, however. The problems involved are essentially those of any Out party in its effort to get In. There is little evidence of significant partisan bias in the present system.

Finally, political apathy supposedly engendered under the electoral system is a prime target of some reformers. Yet the system is not in any real sense responsible for whatever apathy may exist. Moreover, the voter turnout for presidential elections tends to be significantly higher than for other elections. In addition, the relative political stability that has been maintained in the United States under the electoral college system is promoted by the nonideological, often low-key politics (which often passes for apathy) that the system does encourage.

Others oppose the present electoral vote system because they believe that state boundaries ought to be abolished for purposes of presidential elections. An academic argument can be made for such a change. But should state boundaries also be abolished for presidential nominations? For congressional elections? For purposes of subnational governmental administration? Should the federal system be moved toward a unitary state? In this vast, variable, and populous land it seems doubtful. To eliminate state units in presidential voting would set an injudicious precedent.

Furthermore, there is little concrete evidence that such a change is needed. Aggregating the popular vote by states has not deprived the popular vote winner of the presidency since 1888. It seems far less likely to do so today. We have concluded that the principal reason for divergence between popular and electoral votes has been the one-party states, where a candidate can roll up a large margin of popular votes while narrowly losing the electoral vote bloc of more competitive states. Yet in the 1960s there were far fewer one-party states than in the 1880s; and they accounted for a smaller percentage of the total electoral vote, of the total popular vote, and of the total popular vote of each party than they did in the 1880s. As the one-party states have declined in number, so has the possibility of a runner-up President under the existing system. Historically, the system has, since 1888, provided the popular plurality winner with an electoral vote majority, which has given him a strong position from which to begin to exercise the powers of the presidency.

Finally, remote contingencies that may affect elections under the existing system are often criticized. It would be unfortunate if they had any real impact, but in fact their modest significance has been vastly magnified in the course of the policy debate. In addition, solutions to problems such as succession in the case of death have been easily arranged within the present system.

The existing electoral system has for almost two centuries produced Presidents widely acceptable to the variegated groups that comprise the American citizenry. It has strengthened the presidential mandate to govern. It has been a prime support of the national two-party system in America. It has contributed to the viability of the federal system of government. In all its complexity, the electoral system manages to give appropriate weight to a great many of the relevant factors in American political life. The heaviest weight remains the will of the voters. The next most important is the will of the state units. The will of the major metropolitan areas, which are the most heterogeneous places in the country and are seriously underrepresented elsewhere in the political system, receives important attention. This system produces a rough kind of justice. But it is a kind of justice that seems to work.

The Automatic Plan

What of the alternatives? Essentially, the automatic plan would keep the electoral vote system with the general-ticket system but would eliminate the possibility that an elector might vote for someone other than his party's nominee. This would strengthen the dominant group within each of the major parties and also lock in other aspects of the present system. Additional provisions included in some automatic plans would provide various contingency election procedures to be used if there is no electoral vote majority, as well as procedures to be followed if a candidate dies or there is a tie.

The automatic plan has much to commend it. For reasons already stated, we favor continuing the electoral vote system with the state general-ticket system. In addition to making those systems mandatory, the automatic plan would write into the Constitution a requirement that electoral votes be cast in accordance with the popular vote outcome in each state. The plan would also give Congress power to regulate presidential elections comparable to the power it has to regulate congressional elections. It would improve the contingency election procedures. All of these changes would be desirable, except for the popular runoff provisions contained in some proposed automatic plans.

However, the case for the automatic plan is not totally compelling as an argument for a constitutional amendment. The plan would close loopholes, but they are loopholes that have made little difference in American history. Moreover, the political parties, since they draw up the slates, could take steps to correct the problems concerning electors. In addition, there is the risk that to the beneficial features of the automatic plan might be added some undesirable changes—notably a popular runoff contingency election or abolition of the general-ticket system. Any number of potentially dangerous provisions might be written into any constitutional amendment on this subject, particularly at a time when so many divergent proposals are being put forth in Congress. The most desirable electoral systems would be either the automatic plan with a contingency election choice of the President from the top two candidates by a majority vote of either the House (with the Senate choosing the Vice President) or a joint session of Congress; or the automatic plan with designation of the popular vote winner as President if no one gets an electoral majority. A popular runoff election in the context of the automatic plan, while preferable to a runoff in conjunction with other proposed systems, would be an undesirable change because of its adverse effects on the party system and the presidency.

The main question about the automatic plan remains: Does its modest change in the existing system justify the labor and risk of a constitutional amendment?

The District Plan

The three remaining methods of electing the President would all abolish the general-ticket system, thus bringing about a very different kind of political situation and with it a weakened presidency. Although, like the automatic plan, the district plan would require that each electoral vote go to the candidate its constituency chose, the district plan would drastically localize presidential elections. Most electoral votes would come from local single-elector districts. Since state legislatures would establish the district lines, this plan would strengthen state governments in relation to the national government. States that do not contain major metropolitan areas would particularly gain. The constituency base of the presidency would be made to approximate that of Congress. The focus of the party system would turn to local areas. It appears that minor parties, Republicans, and conservatives generally would benefit from the district plan.

The plan aims to change the existing balance of power in presidential elections, particularly the metropolitan bias, by eliminating the state general-ticket system. In its present form the plan would also serve, in much the same fashion as does the automatic plan, to assure that the electoral votes go to the national parties' candidates and to deal with problems of the contingency election, with tie-votes, and with the death of a candidate. The merits of these changes have already been discussed. Its unique change, the localization of presidential elections, we consider extremely undesirable. At present, the focus of presidential attention is fundamentally national. It should be. The President (together with the Vice President) is the only public official in the United States who is elected by a nationwide vote. He presides over one of the largest and most diverse countries in the world; among nations of its size in both population and area, it is the only one whose people actually elect such a leader. The complexities of the system under which the President governs require that he always give consideration to the state and local aspects of major policy decisions. The existence of the federal system and of the locally oriented Congress assures that he will. "District" interests are adequately represented by members of the Senate and, particularly, by members of the House of Representatives. The President needs to have the fundamental freedom to act as a national leader. Under the district plan he would be more oriented toward local and state concerns than he is under the existing system. Congress, and the state and local interests it represents, would become preeminent, and interests that are essentially national would suffer a corresponding decline.

Perhaps what the proponents of the district plan really have in mind is that some states and localities do not receive what they think is adequate attention under the present election system. They would argue that the President's "real" constituency today lies in the major metropolitan areas and the populous states in which they are located. This diagnosis is largely correct; these areas *are* crucial to the presidency. But they should be. We have already pointed to their needs and the lack of attention given them elsewhere in the political system, as well as to the moderating tendency of their voters to favor the same presidential candidates as does the country as a whole. Furthermore, their problems are inextricably linked with those of other Americans, particularly residents of small town and rural areas, whose spokesmen tend to resent most the metropolitan bias of the existing system. Competition for attention is inevitable. But ultimately the issue is national; and it will take national leadership, particularly from the President, to deal with it.

The Proportional Plan

Under the proportional plan, the electoral college would be abolished, but state electoral votes would be retained. Each state's electoral votes would be divided among the candidates in proportion to the popular vote in the state. Thus the plan would aggregate votes by parties by states. If no candidate received at least 40 percent of the national electoral vote total, Congress in joint session would choose the President.

Like all plans that abolish the general-ticket system, the proportional plan would undermine the two-party system, eliminate the present advantage of major metropolitan areas in the most populous states, and weaken the presidential mandate to govern. In addition, the possibility of prolonged indecision in close contests would be increased; a complex counting process, difficult to follow, would be established.

Supporters of this plan claim that it is the only way to assure relative equality of voting power for all citizens within the context of the federal system. The plan does retain a degree of state autonomy in presidential elections and, with its precise mathematical requirements, would appear at first glance to reflect the popular will more faithfully than does the present system. But not necessarily. Each state would still have at least three electoral votes; the number of its additional electoral votes would still be based on outdated population figures rather than on voter turnout, and as a result the state-by-state proportional figures would not necessarily equal the nationwide totals. However, the present electoral system has always elected the popular winner in the twentieth century and seems very likely to continue doing so.

The proportional plan suffers from another serious deficiency. It would be divisive. Its very method emphasizes the precise proportional division of voter sentiment. Moreover, under it, parties would tend to be more homogeneous and ideological, and it would encourage "spoilers." Its divisiveness would be a particularly serious drawback in periods of severe national unrest.

The Direct-Vote Plan

The direct-vote plan would abolish the entire electoral vote system and replace it with election by a nationwide popular vote. Under a plan approved by the House, the candidate receiving the most popular votes would be elected provided he received 40 percent of the total; if he did not, a popular runoff election between the top two candidates would be held. The President and Vice President would be elected as a ticket. Congress would be empowered to deal with a candidate's death or withdrawal.

Under the direct-vote plan, populous states and their major metropolitan areas would be less powerful in presidential elections and perhaps in presidential policymaking than they are under the present system. The party system would change dramatically. Minor parties would gain votes, since they would now "count." Although local minor parties would lose their swing-vote leverage, national minor parties (notably spoilers) would be strengthened. With more minor parties, politics would tend to be more ideological, since popular issues would be a principal basis of such parties. With more issue-oriented campaigns, the electorate might become more politicized. Especially with a popular runoff system, elections would be more costly. In both major parties, progressive elements, usually representing metropolitan areas, would stand to lose. The President, who would frequently be elected with less than a majority and perhaps only after a runoff contest, would be weakened. Political instability would be more likely. National administration of presidential elections would probably be necessary.

The direct-vote plan could do great damage to the national two-party system that the electoral college system has promoted. One of the major stabilizing influences in U.S. political history has come from focusing the presidential contest on the competing strengths of two great national parties, each hugging the center of national political forces. The two-party system is not an invulnerable arrangement; it is, in fact, quite vulnerable to the particular incentives to multiparty competition that the direct-vote plan would create.

The most serious risk under the direct-vote plan results from its heavy dependence on contingency election procedures. One of the strongest virtues of the existing electoral college system is that it has rarely been necessary to resort to the contingency provisions for electing the President. This has tended to legitimize the new President in the eyes of the Washington and world communities with which he must work when he governs. The direct-vote plan, with its provision for a runoff election if no candidate receives at least 40 percent of the popular vote, would probably provide a powerful incentive for third and fourth parties. Their aims would be to reduce the top candidate's lead to less than 40 percent, thus forcing a runoff election in which the minor party leaders could bargain advantageously with either the runner-up or the leading candidate. Under the direct-vote plan, runoff elections would probably become the strategic objective of all participants in the presidential contest except those who supported the acknowledged leading candidate (if there were such a candidate). It is not difficult to forecast the hazards to the American political system of even occasional runoff elections for President: prolonged uncertainty about the election outcome, rumors of "deals" and "bargains," loss to the President of an untarnished mandate, his consequently low standing with the public and with Washington and international policymakers, a weak President with a fixed four-year term. Nor can direct-vote plan advocates escape their dilemma by abolishing the 40-percent plurality target; to do so would merely increase the likelihood of Presidents with weak, disputed mandates to govern.

Of all the probable effects, the one most stressed by advocates of the direct vote is the theoretical equality of each citizen at the ballot box. While some advocates of the direct vote strongly favor abolishing the state general-ticket system, most of them stress the one-person-one-vote aspects of their plan. They view the matter as one of political justice. Political consequences, they argue, are secondary. The real question, in their opinion, is whether or not one vote shall be as powerful as any other in choosing the President of the United States.

This argument greatly oversimplifies the issue. It ignores some probably profound political effects and violates the sound rule that no policy decision, least of all one so centrally involved with the distribution of national political power, should be made in a political vacuum. Moreover, the direct-vote plan is not a logical extension of the one-person-one-vote doctrine of the Supreme Court reapportionment decisions.[1] Those cases concerned variations in the population basis for drawing the boundaries of legislative districts. The idea was that, in addition to other criteria, the districts should have relatively equal numbers of inhabitants. The direct-vote plan for electing the President, in contrast, would not use *population* as the basis for aggregating votes; instead, it would use *voters* who cast valid ballots at the polls. Thus, the standard employed would not be one-person-one-vote or one-citizen-one-vote or even one-adult-citizen-one-vote, but rather one-voter-one-vote. The familiar slogan so often used in behalf of the direct-vote plan is not conceptually appropriate even to the plan's objectives.

In a more practical sense, the premise that each vote cast can somehow be made to be exactly equal to every other vote cast is a shaky one. Such absolute equality is impossible to achieve under any political system; it is clearly impossible in a complex nation of more than 200 million people. Electoral politics is based largely on symbolic appeals to voting groups. In attempting to build a successful coalition, leaders must always stress certain segments of the population more than others. They concentrate their efforts

1. See the cases cited in Chap. 2.

where they think they will do the most good—on groups of voters who tend to vote alike, on their own partisans, and on independents. Under any electoral system, some voters are "more equal" than others—not only to political leaders, but to the voters themselves. Those voting for a losing candidate will always have a tendency to claim disfranchisement, whatever the level at which the votes are aggregated. If they do not like the winner's subsequent performance in office, they can always point out that they did not vote for him; in any case, they can contend with some justification that he does not really represent *them*. The President who is elected, of course, *does* represent them and indeed all Americans; but in the sense of "standing for"[2] them, he represents them less than he does those who voted for him.

The central issue in evaluating the various electoral systems is the nature of the most desirable presidential constituency. The existing system, in aggregating the vote by states, demands a balance among several relevant factors. It produces a slight variation from the popular outcome, but its added virtues make it preferable to any simple popular vote system. Under the present arrangement, the popular choice wins; but the states play an important role, and the metropolitan areas receive particular attention. The direct-vote plan is based on voters as voters, with no weighting for the state and metropolitan factors. It would legitimize a far narrower constituency base. Particularly at a time when the nation is divided as rarely before with dissension on vital issues, the wisdom of a broad consensus is apparent. Proponents of the direct-vote plan are right in believing that in order to govern effectively, a President needs a strong popular mandate; they err in their judgment of the kind of mandate that is strongest. In modern American history that mandate has always come from the voters at large, the mandate based on consensus registered through the electoral vote system.

2. See Hanna F. Pitkin, *The Concept of Representation* (University of California Press, 1967), Chap. 4.

Recommendations

This analysis leads us to make the following policy suggestions:

1. The electoral vote system with the general-ticket system should be retained. It is not perfect. But its defects are known, and they are relatively minor. The defects of the proposed alternatives are uncertain, and they appear to the authors to be major.

Most grievances against the existing system can be resolved through the political process without recourse to a constitutional amendment. It is preferable that desirable adaptations be brought about, as they have been in the past, by means other than the amendment procedure. If it is believed that some constitutional amendment must be passed, the most prudent choice would be the automatic plan, with a required electoral vote majority and the general-ticket system, and the provision that in a contingency election the President should be chosen (a) from the top two candidates by majority vote in either the House or a joint session of Congress, or (b) by designation as President and Vice President of the ticket winning the popular vote. In broad outline, this plan would continue the essential characteristics of the existing electoral college system.

2. Within the present electoral college system, national party leaders should take the steps necessary to ensure loyalty from state electors of their party. They can minimize the problem of the "faithless" elector by seeing that more care is taken in the selection of individual electors. They can call for loyalty resolutions at national party conventions. The sanctions of national patronage, campaign funds, and general support are at their disposal. In short, they have the opportunity to bargain for the selection of responsible and loyal electors. In some instances, leaders have made such efforts, often with success. The failure to secure faithful electors has frequently been the result of insufficient attention on the part of national leaders. Their success in assuring loyal electors depends largely upon their own skill, but a continuing effort is required;

frenetic, last-minute efforts every four years may be too little and too late. To this end, regular, routinized communications among national, state, and local party leaders would be desirable. National party leaders and staff members could work to assure that the names of their presidential and vice presidential candidates or full slates of electors loyal to their candidates are on the ballot in each state.

3. If, under the existing procedures, an election appears to be so close that a winner seems doubtful even in the House, there are opportunities for responsible negotiations and prior (even continuing) agreements. For example, House members could agree— as some did in 1968—to elect the popular winner if the electoral vote system failed to produce a President. The Senate could agree to do the same in choosing a Vice President.

4. An important procedural matter that should be resolved is the problem of what to do if a candidate dies or is otherwise incapacitated. The national party organizations should continue to take responsibility in this area by adopting a rule dealing with this possibility at each national convention. The parties have shown commendable foresight in adopting such resolutions in the past. Candidates for national office are political, rather than governmental, leaders; and the line of succession to their posts should accordingly be determined by the political party organizations.

5. Similarly, the states should deal with the possibility that an elector may be unable to carry out his function. Some states already have passed laws covering this possibility; and those that have not should do so.

We believe that with these improvements, the electoral college could continue and expand the benefits it has provided the American political system. Although imperfect, as Hamilton predicted, the electoral college system has at least been excellent. It has worked well. It has evolved along with the nation and has in every era produced Presidents accepted as legitimate and capable of governing effectively. It has been a salutary force in American politics, in ways of which Hamilton never dreamed. It has encouraged political leaders to wage their struggles within two great parties. It has provided a point of access for metropolitan interests that are often ignored elsewhere. It has promoted national stability in the battle for the presidency. We see no reason to abandon, and many reasons to support, an institution whose assets have been very tangible and whose liabilities have been largely conjectural.

Appendix

CONFERENCE DISCUSSION OF ALTERNATIVE PLANS

A BROOKINGS conference of experts assembled on February 6, 1969, to consider an early draft of this book. While no formal canvass of views was made, a consensus was evident about the necessary components of an ideal presidential election system and about the main theme of the book—that any electoral system significantly affects the broader political system. Controversy developed over more specific issues: the particular effects of specific electoral systems on the party system and on the presidency itself; the extent of danger arising under the existing system from faithless electors; the relative merits of various contingency election schemes; considerations of political strategy and tactics in electoral reform; and the fundamental question of which plan for electing the President is best.

An Ideal Presidential Election System

Four criteria, some of which tend to conflict, were accepted by the conferees as components of an ideal system for electing the President and Vice President:

First, the election procedure should guarantee, insofar as possible, a quick election decision with a clear-cut winner. The possibility of a period of "constitutional crisis," during which the identity of the victor is uncertain, should be eliminated or at least minimized.

Second, the system should be democratic. "The people's choice," the man with the most popular votes, should win.

Third, the President should be "legitimate," as defined by twentieth-century conceptions of democracy in the United States. He should have a margin of votes sufficient to be generally considered a "popular mandate to govern." Precise parameters of legitimacy have never been established. An acceptable mandate is a margin of victory somewhere between a *plurality* of one vote and a *majority* of one vote.

Finally, the system should not undermine accepted norms of American politics, particularly the two-party system.

Electoral Systems and the Broader Political System

No participant in the conference disputed the authors' assumption that the method of electing the President affects the American political system as a whole. There was a cautious tendency on the part of one or two scholars not to ascribe too much to the presidential electoral system and too little to other variables. In addition, at least one proponent of the direct-vote plan considered political effects merely speculative and secondary to the principle of a one-person-one-vote popular election of the President. There was general agreement, however, that the political consequences of various plans should be carefully considered in the policy debate.

THE PARTY SYSTEM

Specifically, the conferees discussed at length the effects of presidential electoral systems on the political party system. There was wide agreement that the method of choosing the President affects the number and kind of parties. At issue were two questions: whether the electoral system is an independent or a dependent variable, and whether the presidential electoral system or the congressional electoral system is more significant.

One participant emphasized that the broad political culture is probably the most relevant variable. The electoral college system may have acted as a "brake" rather than as an "accelerator" for minor party movements, he said; but these movements usually arose during periods of social tension, when many citizens were unable or unwilling to identify with the major parties. Another scholar objected to any sharp distinction between political culture and the electoral system. He argued that each of these factors affects the other.

Others questioned whether the method of choosing the President is the most important influence on the party system. It was noted that many academic studies have identified the election of House members from single-member districts on a simple plurality basis as the major determinant of a two-party system. Most participants in the Brookings conference, however, were unwilling to conclude that the presidential electoral system has no significant impact on party activity. Indeed, the possible effects of the direct-vote plan on the party system was the central concern of many political scientists at the meeting.

As to specific plans, most participants agreed that the present electoral vote system, with the general-ticket system, discourages minor parties because they must carry whole states in order to be effective. Most of the conferees also agreed that the direct-vote plan would encourage more present or potential minor parties to enter the presidential contest because they would have more impact on the national outcome. One dissenter, however, viewed the present system as the more vulnerable because of possible threats from regional minor parties.

Again, though the panel of experts agreed that any presidential election system significantly affects the nominating process, they diverged in their assessments of specific plans. One political scientist went so far as to reject all speculation about what would have occurred in past elections under alternative methods of electing the President, because under other plans the parties might have nominated different candidates. Several others agreed that such projections are unreliable. Again, one participant contended that the direct-vote plan would bring about "an ad hoc reform of the nominating process," in which a candidate's popularity with rank-and-file voters would become more important in choosing nominees. Others pointed to the consensus-building aspects of the existing electoral vote system: the need to nominate a ticket acceptable to the major factions of each major party. One professor emphasized that a balanced ticket, and not merely a President, is chosen under the electoral college system; the nature of that system, she contended, determined the nature of the balancing to create a ticket.

THE PRESIDENCY AS AN INSTITUTION: LEGITIMACY AND GOVERNANCE

Concern with presidential legitimacy was a recurrent theme of the discussion. The participants agreed that a President must be considered legitimate, or he cannot govern; they also agreed that his electoral margin affects the extent of his legitimacy and hence the initial base from which he exercises the powers of office. The conferees could not agree, however, about the exact boundaries of presidential legitimacy.

The legitimacy question was closely related to what kind of contingency election, if any, there should be. The conferees agreed that use of contingency elections should be kept at a minimum, and they agreed that the legitimacy of Presidents with a low plurality is likely to be dubious. What they could not agree on was the most appropriate way of counting the votes in close elections.

When is a President "legitimate"? Conferees disagreed. One sanguine participant observed that most voters voted against President Nixon in 1968 but nonetheless accepted him as the legitimate President because he was elected under the rules of the game. The implication was that Americans are willing to abide by any rules so long as they are fairly reasonable. Other conferees argued, however, that there are limits to this tolerance; if, for example, there were ever a runner-up President, popular resentment would lead to a change in the system. Again, the argument was made and generally accepted that even the largest election mandate does not assure that a President can govern effectively for four years; Lyndon Johnson was cited as a case in point.

"Dangers" in the Existing System

There was considerable discussion of the supposed faults of the existing system. The conferees debated particularly the extent of the threat posed by possibly disloyal human electors and the merits of various contingency election procedures.

FAITHLESS ELECTORS

The conferees did not agree completely about the magnitude of the threat posed by possibly faithless electors. While no one thought it desirable for electors to frustrate the popular will, many did not consider the danger very serious. But this view was not unanimous. One participant found it profoundly undemocratic that conceivably "a handful of men" could change the outcome of the election. Most of his colleagues, however, seemed more impressed by the statistic that only six of more than 16,000 electors since 1789 have been unfaithful.

Still, there was evident within the group considerable dissatisfaction with the idea of human electors. There were no objections to the proposition that the automatic registering of a state's electoral votes for its popular winner was preferable to entrusting this task to any group of possibly independent-minded officials. One participant labeled the notion of an electoral college a "Whig concept," with unpledged electors as an extreme example of Whiggery.

CONTINGENCY ELECTIONS

Much of the discussion concerned the way a President should be chosen if the ordinary election procedure did not produce a winner. Three methods were debated by the conferees: election by a simple popular plurality, by a popular majority in a runoff contest, and by a majority vote of Congress.

The conferees agreed that a provision for a popular runoff would make contingency elections more likely and that the existing electoral vote system, with the general-ticket system, makes them less likely. They also agreed that an ideal arrangement would make resort to a contingency election as rare as possible. Little satisfaction was expressed with any of the contingency election provisions that have been devised.

Only a few conferees supported a one-shot winner-take-all, *popular plurality* contest. Those who did, argued that the popular verdict could be rendered decisively, with no possible recriminations that the "real" popular favorite had somehow lost in a second contest. Many participants feared, however, that the percentage of the total vote that the winner might receive under a simple plurality system could be very low—perhaps well below 40 percent—thus impairing his legitimacy and his mandate to govern. Others argued that low pluralities would not be the usual result, as they have not been in popular elections of state governors. However, there appeared to be a consensus that, particularly with the direct-vote plan, "legitimate" margins would not necessarily be assured and that opinion leaders have many serious apprehensions about election by an open plurality with no provision at all for a contingency election.

The second major option considered by the conferees was a requirement that, to be elected, a candidate must win some fixed percentage of the electoral or popular vote, with a *popular runoff* if no one achieved the necessary margin. There was wide agreement among the participants that popular runoff elections are undesirable, mainly because they encourage minor parties to wage "spoiler" campaigns.

Many voiced fear that a popular runoff would splinter the political parties. Thus, one political scientist said that minor party leaders would successfully urge many voters to vote their real convictions on the first ballot, since they would have a second choice in the runoff. Most conferees agreed with this analysis.

Two or three participants took different positions. One held that the splinter-party argument ascribed too much influence to the electoral system; the existence or absence of a runoff provision, he said, might encourage or discourage minor parties, but it would hardly determine the extent of their activity. Another conferee contended that the strong two-party tradition would overwhelm minor parties even with a runoff.

On balance, the group rejected the popular runoff idea. There was mild support from one or two proponents of the direct-vote plan who felt that, to be consistent, any contingency election device attached to their plan must be based on a popular vote. However, with one or two exceptions, the direct-vote plan supporters in the group preferred the open plurality system. Two others were willing to entertain the idea that perhaps Congress should be given standby powers to conduct a runoff if necessary.

The third proposal, *choice by Congress*, was viewed by the conferees with little enthusiasm. Some participants did prefer it to the available alternatives if some changes were made in the existing system.

Generally, the group was highly critical of past congressional involvement in the choice of a President, including the extralegal procedure of 1876–77 as well as the constitutionally prescribed House and Senate contingency elections. The obvious problems were pointed out: that the choice of Congress would not necessarily be the popular choice, and that Congress might begin controlling Presidents. Some conferees simply did not think Congress had any business picking a President, and said so.

Several ways of improving the existing system were suggested. Narrowing the choice from the top three candidates to the top two and voting by individual members of Congress rather than by state delegations were both endorsed by individual conferees without discussion or apparent dissent. However, there was disagreement about the desirability of a joint session of Congress to choose both the President and the Vice President. One participant preferred keeping the Senate, two-thirds of whose members would have been chosen two or four years previously, out of the contingency election of the President. Another argued that a comparable percentage of House members are equally unresponsive to current popular thinking. A third view was that the choice of President and Vice President by separate houses of Congress would be more likely to produce someone to assume command on Inauguration Day.

Political Strategy and Tactics

The conferees disagreed about the political costs and benefits of constitutional reform in the presidential electoral system, debating especially whether the small changes that would be involved in adopting the automatic plan justified a constitutional amendment. A second issue, considered more briefly but of equal political significance, was whether reform-minded intellectuals should support the electoral college reform plan that seemed best to them or the plan with most popular support.

Most participants agreed that adoption of the automatic plan would bring desirable improvements: specific congressional control over presidential elections, a better contingency election procedure, federal guarantees of voting rights for all, and the short ballot. However, as one or two conferees noted, adoption of an automatic plan might bring such undesirable changes as abolition of the general-ticket system, a worse contingency election plan, and so on.

In a different context, a direct-vote plan advocate argued that calculations of this sort should be disregarded. He said that political feasibility and fine intellectual technicalities should not take precedence over popular support for the direct-vote plan. Several conferees who supported that plan agreed with his contention that the time had passed when any other kind of reform, and indeed any other kind of system, was acceptable to the people at large. Nonetheless, there appeared to be widespread agreement within the group that details of reform, such as the relative merits of various contingency election plans, might be of great policy significance, and that they were a legitimate concern of political scientists and other scholars seeking to make public policy recommendations.

The Best Plan

The conferees were divided in their judgment as to which particular system for electing the President is best. Most of them would have preferred to see some reform, especially in the contingency election system, but doubted the likelihood of any such limited reform. There was strong support within the group for the electoral vote system with the general-ticket system. There was also substantial support for the direct-vote plan; most of its proponents among the conferees preferred a straight plurality rule, without any popular runoff arrangement. There was no real support for the district or proportional plans, though at least one direct-vote advocate was willing to go along with the proportional plan as the next best alternative.

CONFERENCE PARTICIPANTS

ERNEST J. BROWN *Harvard University Law School*

WILLIAM NISBET CHAMBERS *Washington University*

PAUL T. DAVID *University of Virginia*

JOHN A. DAVIS *City University of New York*

CHARLES E. GILBERT *Brookings Institution and Swarthmore College*

MARIAN D. IRISH *American University*

JAMES C. KIRBY, JR. *New York University Law School*

SAMUEL KRISLOV *University of Minnesota*

GARY ORFIELD *University of Virginia*

JUDITH H. PARRIS *Brookings Institution*

NEAL R. PEIRCE Congressional Quarterly

WALLACE S. SAYRE *Columbia University*

RICHARD C. SCAMMON *Governmental Affairs Institute*

RUTH C. SILVA *Pennsylvania State University*

GILBERT Y. STEINER *Brookings Institution (Chairman)*

DONALD E. STOKES *University of Michigan*

SELECTED BIBLIOGRAPHY

Articles

Banzhaf, John F., III. "One Man, 3.312 Votes: A Mathematical Analysis of the Electoral College," *Villanova Law Review*, Vol. 13 (Winter 1968).

Brown, Ernest J. "Proposed Amendment a Power Vacuum for Political Blackmail?" *Trial*, June–July 1967.

Burns, James MacGregor. "A New Course for the Electoral College," *New York Times Magazine*, December 18, 1960.

David, Paul T. "Reforming the Presidential Nominating Process," *Law and Contemporary Problems*, Vol. 27 (Spring 1962).

Dixon, Robert G., Jr. "Electoral College Procedure," *Western Political Quarterly*, Vol. 3 (June 1950).

Feerick, John D. "The Electoral College—Why It Ought To Be Abolished," *Fordham Law Review*, Vol. 37 (October 1968).

Goodwin, Richard N. "Electoral College Finds a Defender," *Washington Post*, October 5, 1969.

Johnson, Gerald W. "Leave the College Alone," *New Republic*, Vol. 144 (January 9, 1961).

Joyner, Conrad, and Ronald Pedderson. "The Electoral College Revisited," *Southwestern Social Science Quarterly*, Vol. 45 (June 1964).

Kefauver, Estes. "The Electoral College: Old Reforms Take On a New Look," *Law and Contemporary Problems*, Vol. 27 (Spring 1962).

Kirby, James C., Jr. "Limitations on the Power of State Legislatures Over Presidential Elections," *Law and Contemporary Problems*, Vol. 27 (Spring 1962).

Kristol, Irving, and Paul Weaver. "A Bad Idea Whose Time Has Come," *New York Times Magazine*, November 23, 1969.

Lewis, Anthony. "The Case Against Electoral Reform," *The Reporter*, Vol. 10 (December 8, 1960).

Meyer, Donald A. "The Demise of the Independent Elector," *ABA Journal*, Vol. 50 (June 1964).

"Moves to Change the U.S. Electoral System," *Congressional Digest*, Vol. 46 (November 1967).

"New Interest Shown in Reform of Electoral System," *Congressional Quarterly Weekly Report*, Vol. 19 (February 17, 1961).

Orfield, Gary. "A Proposal for Outfoxing Wallace," *Washington Post*, July 7, 1968.

Peirce, Neal R. "The Electoral College Goes to Court," *The Reporter*, Vol. 35 (October 6, 1966).

Roche, John P. "The Electoral College: A Note on American Political Mythology," *Dissent* (Spring 1961).

———. "The Founding Fathers: A Reform Caucus in Action," *American Political Science Review*, Vol. 55 (December 1961).

Rogers, Lindsay, and William Y. Elliott. "Shall We Abolish the Electoral College?" *Forum*, Vol. 97 (January 1937).

Silva, Ruth C. "The Lodge-Gossett Resolution: A Critical Analysis," *American Political Science Review*, Vol. 44 (March 1950).

———. "Reform of the Electoral System," *Review of Politics*, Vol. 14 (July 1952).

———. "State Law on the Nomination, Election, and Instruction of Presidential Electors," *American Political Science Review*, Vol. 42 (July 1948).

Sindler, Allan P. "Presidential Election Methods and Urban-Ethnic Interests," *Law and Contemporary Problems*, Vol. 27 (Spring 1962).

"State Power to Bind Presidential Electors," *Columbia Law Review*, Vol. 65 (April 1965).

Wilmerding, Lucius, Jr. "Reform of the Electoral System," *Political Science Quarterly*, Vol. 44 (March 1949).

Wroth, L. Kinvin. "Election Contests and the Electoral Vote," *Dickinson Law Review*, Vol. 65 (June 1961).

Books

American Bar Association. *Electing the President: A Report of the Commission on Electoral College Reform*. Chicago: ABA, 1967.

Bean, Louis H. *Ballot Behavior*. Washington: Public Affairs Press, 1961.

Bickel, Alexander M. *The New Age of Political Reform*. New York: Harper & Row, 1968.

Campbell, Angus, and others. *The American Voter*. New York: John Wiley & Sons, 1960.

Duverger, Maurice. *Political Parties.* New York: John Wiley & Sons, 1959.

Heard, Alexander. *A Two-Party South?* Chapel Hill: University of North Carolina Press, 1952.

Key, V. O., Jr. *Politics, Parties and Pressure Groups.* 5th ed. New York: Thomas Y. Crowell, 1964.

———. *Southern Politics in State and Nation.* New York: Alfred A. Knopf, Inc., 1949.

MacBride, Roger Lea. *The American Electoral College.* Caldwell, Idaho: The Caxton Printers, Ltd., 1953.

Neustadt, Richard E. *Presidential Power.* New York: John Wiley & Sons, 1960.

O'Neil, Charles A. *American Electoral System.* New York: G. P. Putnam's Sons, 1887.

Peirce, Neal R. *The People's President.* New York: Simon & Schuster, 1968.

Polsby, Nelson W., and Aaron Wildavsky. *Presidential Elections.* 2nd ed. New York: Scribners, 1964.

Wilmerding, Lucius, Jr. *The Electoral College.* New Brunswick: Rutgers University Press, 1958.

Public Documents

U.S. Congress. House. Committee on the Judiciary. *Electoral College Reform.* Hearings. 91 Cong. 1 sess. Washington: Government Printing Office, 1969.

U.S. Congress. Senate. Committee on the Judiciary. *Electing the President.* Hearings. 91 Cong. 1 sess. Washington: Government Printing Office, 1969.

———. *Direct Popular Election of the President.* Report. 91 Cong. 2 sess. Washington: Government Printing Office, 1970.

———. *Election of the President.* Hearings. 89 Cong. 2 sess. and 90 Cong. 1 sess. Washington: Government Printing Office, 1968.

———. *Electoral College Reform.* Hearings. 91 Cong. 2 sess. Washington: Government Printing Office, 1970.

———. *Nomination and Election of President and Vice President and Qualifications for Voting.* Hearings. 87 Cong. 1 sess. Washington: Government Printing Office, 1961.

INDEX